MW00992478

ANNE BONY

furniture & interiors of the 1960s

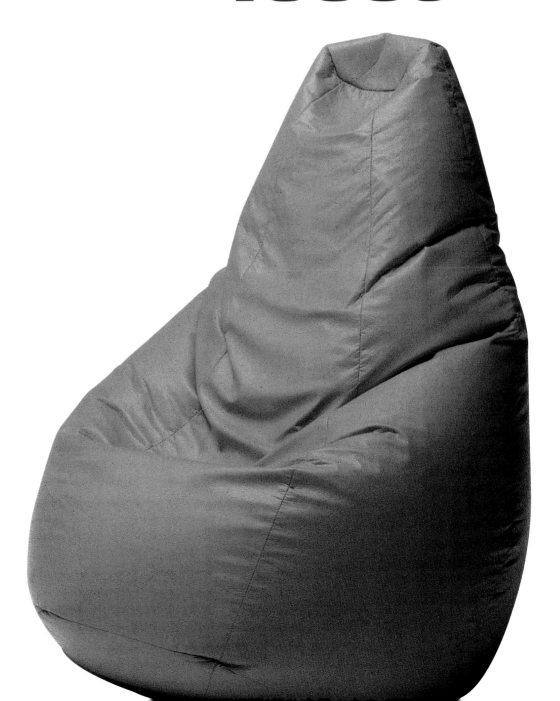

Facing page: Pierre Paulin,
Tongue chair, model 577,
1967. Tubular structure,
foam padding, fabric cover.
Artifort, Schijndel.
Photo: Carol Marc Lavrillier.

Franco Teodoro, Cesare
Paolini, Piero Gatti, Sacco
anatomical chair, 1968.
"Beanbag" filled with
small polystyrene spheres.
Courtesy Zanotta, Milan.
Photo: Masera.

CONTENTS

Facing page: Apartment
interior by Jean-Claude
Maugirard. Dining room
lit with a spectrum
of colors, 1970.
Photo: Pascal Hinous.

Joe Colombo, armchair
model 4801, 1965.
Comprising three
elements in lacquered
molded plywood.
Kartell, Milan.
Courtesy Drouot-Presse,
Paris.

the plastic years

Introduction

Any history of the decorative arts, any study of the styles of the past, brings with it the opportunity to cast further light on the prevailing aesthetics of the period (so often dictated by social imperatives) as well as on the creative careers of individuals. In this respect, the 1960s provides fertile terrain in the sense that the features we will have occasion to analyze here were determined by a social structure of an unprecedented type—consumer society. While the 1950s remained overshadowed by the immediate postwar period, the succeeding decade witnessed the advent of entirely new forms of behavior, new sounds, and new social rules.

The decade from 1960 to 1970 was a turbulent one: nothing was certain, everything was called into question. Through the mass media, television in particular, new ideas and new aspirations reached a wide audience. Consumer society was in the ascendant: the economic crises and recession that would dog the 1970s were yet to come.

Gérard Grandval, desk system with swivel chair made for Jean Bousquet, president of Cacharel, c. 1970.
The unit comprises a system of modular pieces in Plexiglas and plastic.
© Adagp, Paris 2003.

Facing page: Carla Venosta, store interior, c. 1969.
Photo: Carol Marc Lavrillier.

The Pop Years

The 1960s saw the birth of pop culture, a movement that had a considerable impact on both architecture and design. With respect to the 1950s, this new approach to design, which turned the spotlight on the purchasing strategies of the consumer and on the vagaries of fashion, signals a turning point. Design found its expression in the urban tumult, in bright lights, in neon advertising billboards, and in a language which found convenience in everything that fed the Pop Art image bank.

The movement spawned its earliest adepts in Britain, with the Independent Group at the Institute of Contemporary Art in London. The ethics of Pop were consolidated in 1956 on the occasion of the *This is Tomorrow* exhibition organized by the Whitechapel Art Gallery that showcased a substantial number of Pop Art's favorite motifs: Marilyn Monroe, oversized beer bottles, etc.

Inspired by comic strips and advertising, the Pop movement forged a new language in various fields— applied art, interior design, and graphics, as well as in fashion.

Roy Lichtenstein, *M-Maybe*, 1965. Oil on canvas. The Ludwig Collection, Wallraf-Richartz-Museum, Cologne. © Adagp, Paris 2003.

The impact of color was seminal, and designers—spurred on by Roy Lichtenstein, Ellsworth Kelly, Frank Stella, Morris Louis, and Kenneth Noland—turned to a palette of primary colors.

Through its use of the language of mass media, Pop introduced the new consumer culture into art. The pop culture model was that of the individual motivated solely by consumerism, for whom a civilization devoted to his comfort is fostered by mechanisms that stimulate his needs. In this reversal of values, rationalism can no longer be a driving force.

Avant-garde designers in the 1960s duly abandoned any idea of creating exclusive or limited-edition furniture and objects, and directed their efforts instead to manufacturing for the mass market. It was a decade shaped by a new generation: children of the baby boom who had come of age and who now represented potential consumers. They constituted a new target for designers whose prime aim became to manufacture furniture and other goods with a more youthful and colorful look. An anti-materialist spirit defined new rules that dissociated furniture from its former raison d'être: permanence, investment, and longevity. This young customer base brought in its wake a glut of low-priced furniture that fleetingly reflected a new, liberal, and classless way of life.

In the United States, this new take on lifestyle was pushed to its limits, and studies were carried out on the influence of products on the consumers for whom they were intended. A truly popular decorative art thus emerged, and this worship of style is one of the keys to the emergence of pop culture. In 1963, critic Reyner Banham wrote: "The aesthetics of Pop depend on a massive initial impact and small sustaining power and are therefore at their poppiest in products whose sole object is to be consumed". New ways of life, new attitudes: the younger generation was keen to get rid of earlier formalist, classical canons—it preferred to entertain and to share.

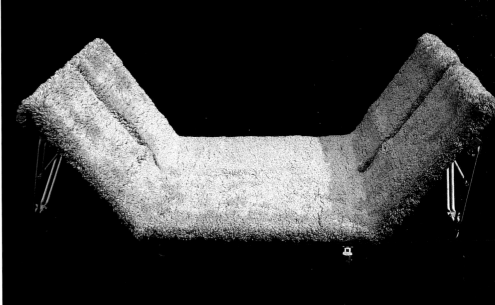

Top: Pierre Paulin, modular Déclive reclining chair, 1968. Foam-covered slats assembled with a linked aluminum chain. Designed for the Mobilier National. Courtesy Galerie de Casson Méron, Paris.

Above: Olivier Mourgue, Tapis reclining chair, 1970. Wooden and metal structure upholstered with woolen carpeting. Courtesy Centre Pompidou, Bibliothèque Kandinsky, Paris. Photo: CCI-DR.

Nanna Ditzel, playground
space with equipment, 1963.
Courtesy Nanna Ditzel.

Nanna Ditzel, set of modular
foam cushions, 1967.
Courtesy Nanna Ditzel.

Facing page: Verner Panton,
Multifunctional Unit, 1966.
Courtesy Verner Panton
Design, Basel.

In 1967 at the Salon des Arts Ménagers, Olivier Mourgue presented the Raft, a large rug with adjustable ends allowing several people to enjoy the unfamiliar sensation of sitting on the floor as comfortably as on a magic carpet. Pierre Paulin exhibited his Tapis Séjour in 1965, soon followed by the Déclive, a structured seat that was mobile, articulated, and adaptable to the moods and requirements of the user. Since happiness was not having to get up, Casati and Hybsch devised a sofa with built-in storage space for magazines and drinks. As space was at a premium, much thought was put into making the best use of what was available. Verner Panton dreamed up "hi-rise housing within the house": users were provided with a vertical structure with levels for different activities—reading, chatting—with hanging, mobile "petal" seats (hammocks) placed at various heights within the dwelling. Joe Colombo erected platforms and daises in apartments to define the volume of the space and its private or communal nature without the use of walls, greater privacy being ensured by lowering the ceiling and by indirect lighting. Nanna Ditzel designed a split-level interior using rostrums, cushions, and color.

The emerging society was one of leisure and enjoyment. The chosen theme of the Thirteenth Milan Triennale in 1964 was "Spare Time." In France and elsewhere, the hub of social life, the café, was being transformed by designers. François Dallegret built a bar in Montreal that looked like a cave, hidden and subterranean. In a Milan hotel, Gae

Aulenti also created an underground space, in the form of a single, continuous, and open reception space. Achille and Piergiacomo Castiglioni installed split-levels and a system of cubicles in a Milan brasserie to ensure a degree of privacy. The Pub Renault was designed in a similar spirit. The changes affecting collective space were international in scope. For the Varna Restaurant in Denmark, Verner Panton proposed an overall design with a pattern over the ceiling and light fixtures, tablecloths, and furniture that matched the carpet.

Nightclubs inspired inventiveness: in Saint-Tropez, with Voom Voom by the architect Paul Bertrand and two major structures by Nicolas Schöffer, and in Nice, where the design at

Bernard Quentin's Blow Club featured an inflatable structure. Francesco and Giancarlo Capolei fitted out a whole series of nightclubs, the Piper in Rome, the Viareggio Piper—a box with plastic-lined walls that was also a fashion boutique—and another Piper in Turin.

Consumer society saw itself reflected in original spaces thought out in new ways. It witnessed the growth of shopping centers, of underground malls, of cities within the city. One of the first malls was designed by Ralph Erskine in Sweden. In France, Claude Parent constructed similar complexes in Ris-Orangis and at Rheims. Certain stores, such as Ideal Standard of Milan, reconsidered their strategy, coming up with environments visible from the

furniture & interiors of the 1960s

street. Artists were a major force behind this way of thinking: Munari, Cinti, Castiglioni, and Gio Ponti. For the Retti candle store in Vienna, Hans Hollein made use of both aluminum and silk. Ugo Pietra, Aldo Jacober, and Paolo Rizzatto introduced further innovations at Altre Cose in Milan: thirty transparent cylinders contained dresses that could be made to move up or down at the touch of a button. In March 1969, the overall design of the new Pierre Cardin store in the Faubourg Saint-Honoré in Paris (with an interior decorated by Nino, Gabrio, and Stefano Bini) amounted to a statement of the brand's new identity.

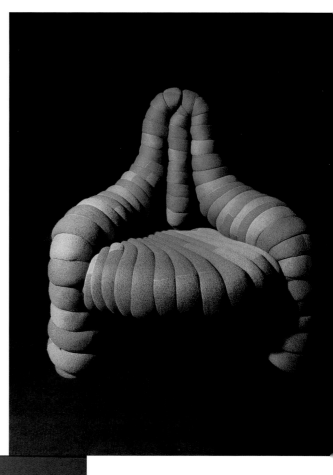

Armchair-sculpture. Tubular structure, upholstered in colored foam rolls.

Verner Panton, Visiona 2, Fantasy Landscape, 1970. Courtesy Verner Panton Design, Basel.

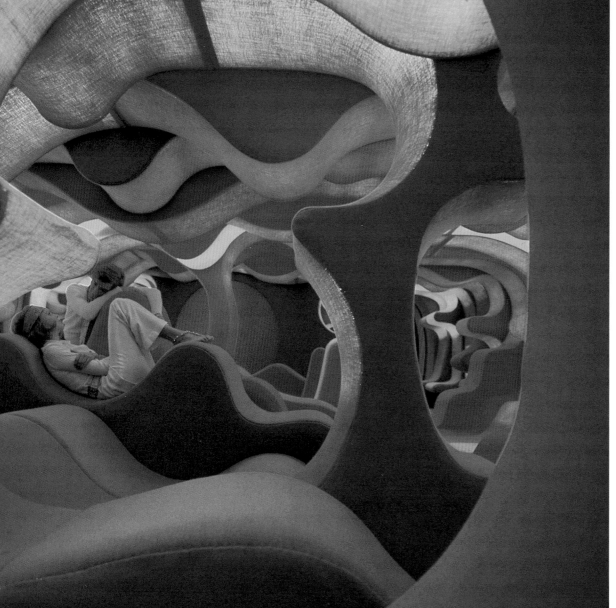

Apartment interior by Jean-Claude Maugirard, 1970. Sliding multifunction storage units. Photo: Pascal Hinous.

Gaetano Pesce, Up 1 series, 1969. Molded polyurethane foam covered in stretch fabric. C&B Italia, Novedrate. Courtesy C&B Italia, Novedrate.

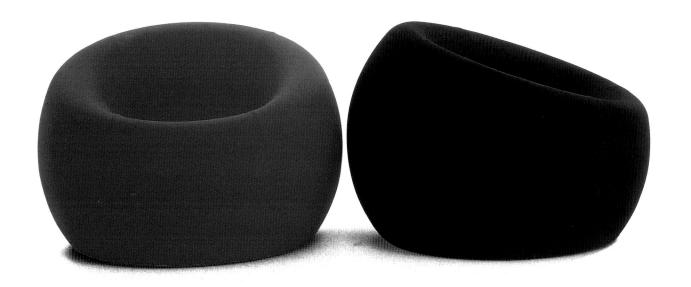

The Plastic Years

The triumph of plastic was one of the outstanding events of the 1960s, and the furniture industry was soon putting the opportunities offered by this low-cost, oil-derived product to good use. Just as plywood had been the material of the 1950s, so the 1960s belonged to ABS, polyethylene, and other thermo-plastics.

These synthetics are strong yet lightweight, lend themselves readily to color treatment, and can be gloss-finished on both sides. While the material was inexpensive, the development of the molds was not. So, when a decision was made to manufacture furniture and objects, this had to be approached on an industrial scale in large quantities to absorb the exorbitant overheads. This marked the onset of relatively cheap and comparatively short-lived production that had to respond to changing fashions and trends.

The concept of fashion modified consumer habits and acted as a spur to the market economy. After studying how consumer industries functioned in the United States, the British artist Richard Hamilton developed and expounded on the theory at the Institute of Contemporary Art in London. The Council of Industrial Design, however, greeted the idea of intensive production of disposable furniture coolly.

Plastic is capable of molecular variations that allow for total freedom in the shapes of furniture. Such materials can be divided into four

Facing page: Joe Colombo, Universale chair, model 4860, 1967. Injection-molded ABS plastic. Kartell, Milan. Photo: Carol Marc Lavrillier.

Jean Dudon, Selle chair, 1970. Double-sided polyester, base at front. Mobilier Moderne. Courtesy Galerie Casson Méron, Paris.

subcategories: ABS, polyurethane foam, PVC, and polyacrylic.

ABS is a rigid plastic that can be injection molded and produced in a single operation. The first country to develop this technique on an industrial scale was Italy, plastic making its debut appearance in an experimental chair by Marco Zanuso and Richard Sapper at the Twelfth Milan Triennale. Marco Zanuso said of the child's chair that won the pair the Compasso d'Oro award in 1964, "This new material, in turn, led to the rethinking of the formal and structural characteristics of the chair... we had created a chair that was also a toy, which would stimulate a child's fantasy... at the same time it was indestructible, and soft enough that it could not harm anyone, yet too heavy to be thrown". (Heisinger and Marcus, *Design Since 1945*, London: Thames & Hudson, 1983).

In 1961, Knoll brought out Richard Schultz's collection, including a plastic seat with an aluminum frame and legs. Vico Magistretti created a collection of tables and chairs manufactured by Artemide. Kartell produced Joe Colombo's experimental variations, notably his stackable chairs. Insatiable innovator that he was, Verner Panton was not one to miss out on such technology, creating and refining his S chair in continuous molded plastic that was manufactured by Herman Miller in 1968. For his part, Finnish designer Eero Aarnio brought out the Pastilli and Globe chairs.

In France, too, many designers exploited this technique but on a smaller, more traditional scale: Marc Held, with his lightweight molded plastic furniture range, including beds, tables, desks, and folding screens; Christian Germanaz, with a form of injected plastic that, in combination, could be manufactured into an armchair, which he presented at the 1968 Milan Triennale.

Polyurethane foam, whose density makes it suitable for cutting, molding or attaching to a frame, allows for great formal freedom. It was also a material that could be shaped, making it possible, for example, to design living spaces without chairs, comprising cushions at various heights, as Jaap Penraat did in 1962. This new approach to living areas was further developed by Bernard Govin at the Société des Artistes Décorateurs in 1966. His recliner was composed of modular foam

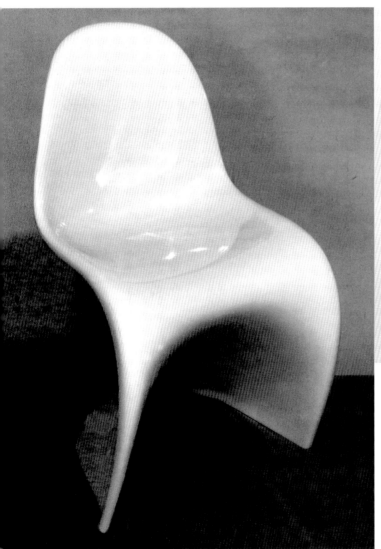

Eero Aarnio, Pastili
armchair, 1968.
Fiberglass-reinforced
polyester.
Asko Lahti, Finland.

Verner Panton, Panton Chair,
1967. Injection-molded
thermoplastic.
Herman Miller Inc., Zeeland.

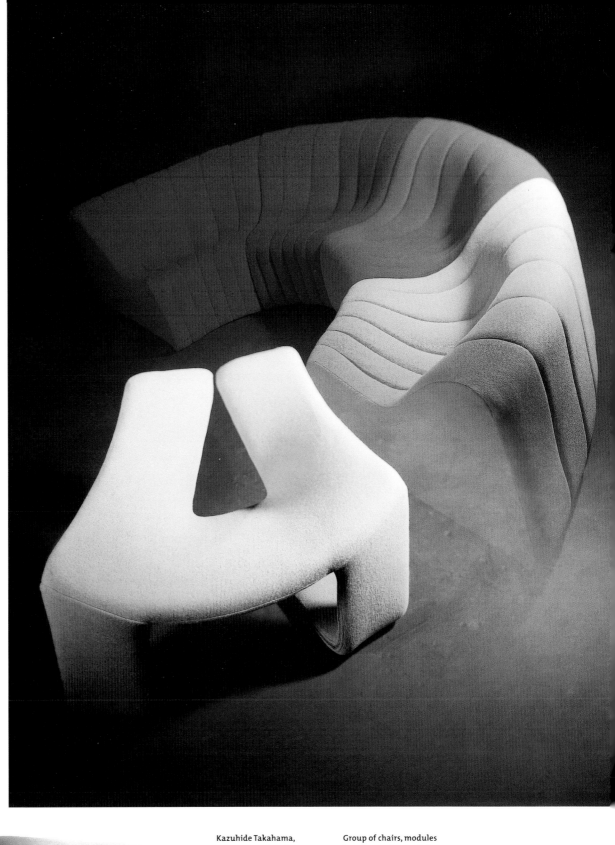

Kazuhide Takahama,
Suzanne armless chair, 1965.
Gavina, Milan.
Courtesy Knoll, New York.

Group of chairs, modules
in various colors and shapes.
Photo: Carol Marc Lavrillier.

by Aubert, Jungmann, and Stinco; and Bernard Quentin an inflatable armchair in yellow, black, or silver. In May 1968, the Eurodomus in Turin was constructed out of inflatable materials designed by Paolo Lomazzi and manufactured by Zanotta.

In the domestic arena, Quasar-Khahn moved with his family into an inflatable interior eighteen feet (six meters) in circumference with walls made out of inflatable tubing, together with inflatable seats and lamps. The whole unit was erected at the *Structures Gonflables* (Inflatable Structures) exhibition at the Musée d'Art Moderne de la Ville de Paris in March 1968, at the Atelier de Recherche et de Création (ARC). The catalog was introduced by an essay entitled "Technologie et société. De considérations inactuelles sur le gonflable et de particularités des structures gonflables" (Technology and society: some untimely reflections on the inflatable and some particularities of inflatable structures); the exhibition was inspired by a journal of urban sociology called *Utopie*, and based on the work of the Aérolande group (Aubert, Jungmann, and Stinco), which presented a range of inflatable furniture kits. In December 1968, Shiro Kuramata exhibited prototypes of invisible plastic furniture and an English fashion collection in a bubble dome. For the 1970 World's Fair in Osaka, the Japanese Fuji pavilion, the brainchild of Yutaka Murata, was an inflatable structure ninety feet (thirty meters) in height.

Thanks to its transparency, polyacrylic (acrylic polymers, such as

Quasar-Khahn, cylindrical inflatable living space, 1967. Assembled vertically from cylindrical elements capped with a circular lens, floor reinforced with a torus band.
© Aérolande, Paris.
Photo: Michel Moch.

Quasar-Khahn, inflatable armchairs, 1968. Courtesy Centre Pompidou, Bibliothèque Kandinsky, Paris.

Jonathan De Pas, Donato
D'Urbino, Paolo Lomazzi,
and Carla Scolari,
Blow chair, 1967.
Inflatable transparent PVC.
Zanotta, Milan.
Courtesy Zanotta, Milan.

Marc Held, Culbuto
armchair, c. 1967.
Fiberglass shell
upholstered and
covered with fabric.
Knoll.
Courtesy Galerie Jousse
Entreprise, Paris.
Photo: Marc Domage.

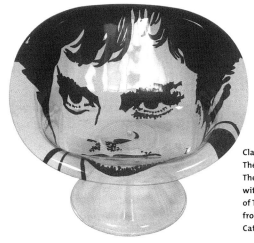

Claude Courtecuisse,
Théorèma chair, 1967.
Thermoformed metacrylate
with silkscreen print
of Terence Stamp's face
from Pasolini's *Theorem*.
Cattanéo.

David Colwell, Contour chair,
1968. Acrylic shell,
chromium-steel frame.
4's Co. Ltd, London.
Courtesy Victoria & Albert
Museum, London.
© V&A Picture Library.

Danielle Quarante,
Albatross chair, 1969.
Resin and polyester.
Airborne, Montreuil.
Courtesy Drouot-Presse,
Paris.
© Adagp, Paris 2003.

Plexiglas, Altuglas, and Perspex) was
a material much appreciated by
designers in their quest for new ways
of understanding space. See-through,
it corresponded to the desire to change
the social fabric, to live in communes,
and bring an end to individual space.
This material was used by Joe Colombo
for a Milan camera store, where the
windows resembled flying saucers.
Finnish designer Yrjö Kukkapuro created
the Karelli chair out of fiberglass, while
Marc Held's Culbuto armchair is made
from polyester with a fiberglass shell.
Olivier Mourgue's figure/chair from
the Bouloum series has a polyester shell
lined with jersey-covered foam.
The Kaleidoscope chair by Jacques
Famery, presented at the Milan
Triennale in 1968, was made out
of Rhodoid (cellulose acetate).

Italian Design

On an industrial scale, the Italians proved to be the most daring and the most talented at employing innovative techniques, materials, and concepts. To compete with Britain and the United States, they decided to invest in research. Designers joined forces in studios and established links with craftsmen and technicians, developing an endless stream of prototypes. Such ateliers acted as breeding grounds for ideas where advances in production technique and the range of shapes might be made. Such new applications offered great freedom in terms of formal creativity and laid the foundations of the Italian "design miracle": the fields affected included furniture, interior design, and object design (glass, light fixtures, ceramics, and accessories). Many companies were launched during the economic boom: Cassina and Busnelli (C&B); Kartell, the company behind Joe Colombo, was founded in 1949; set up in 1956, Poltronova changed tack after its encounter with Ettore Sottsass to become a hive of avant-garde design experiment in which Gae Aulenti, Massimo Vignelli, and Angelo Mangiarotti were to collaborate; Artemide, the lighting company, was awarded the Compasso d'Oro in 1967 for its Eclisse lamp by Vico Magistretti; Zanotta, founded in the 1950s by Aurelia Zanotta, the first to produce and distribute consciously "avant-garde" furniture.

Italian industry also made a notable contribution to the technique of injection molding. Whereas during the Second World War and in the 1950s, plastic's potential had been exploited on a purely utilitarian level, in the 1960s, designers such as Vico Magistretti, Marco Zanuso, and Joe Colombo elevated the material to an altogether higher plane.

One of the forces driving the Italian avant-garde was the promotion of international research to be found in successive issues of the magazine *Domus*. Landmark articles on the Zeitgeist by authors such as Pierre Restany, among others, often appeared in its pages. In what was an exhilarating climate, the magazine sponsored the *Eurodomus* exhibitions organized by Gio Ponti, Giorgio Casati, and Emanuele Ponzio that presented avant-garde solutions to the problem of applying

Facing page: Mario Bellini, Il Tondorante restaurant, 1968. Courtesy Mario Bellini Associati, Milan.

Eugenio Gerli, B 106 minibar, 1966. Tecno, Milan. Courtesy Tecno, Milan.

Achille Castiglioni,
Allunagio garden chair, 1966.
Enamel steel tube structure
and aluminum seat.
Zanotta, Milan.
Courtesy Studio Castiglioni,
Milan.

Apartment interior
by Colin Morrow, 1970.
Adorning a dining room
with curule chairs in
curved Perspex,
the copper base
of the glass table
incorporates a Perspex
aquarium.
Photo: Pascal Hinous.

Below: Hall of an apartment
decorated by Colin Morrow,
1970. On the table, a set
of four Perspex spheres.
Photo: Pascal Hinous.

Facing page: Apartment
interior by Colin Morrow,
1970. The living-room
floor is raised,
the space being
occupied by a large sofa
on a goatskin rug
Photo: Pascal Hinous.

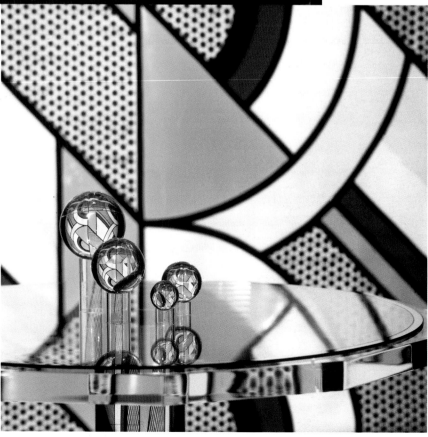

A Jean Bouquin model
photographed in a Plexiglas
armchair, c. 1969.

Lionel Morgaine,
round bathtub.
Courtesy Lionel Morgaine.
Photo: Georges Palot, Paris.

Facing page: Winter garden
by Colin Morrow treated
in white lacquer, 1970.
The furniture is in Perspex;
the day bed is made of
a single sheet of contoured
Perspex with a leather-
covered mattress.
Photo: Pascal Hinous.

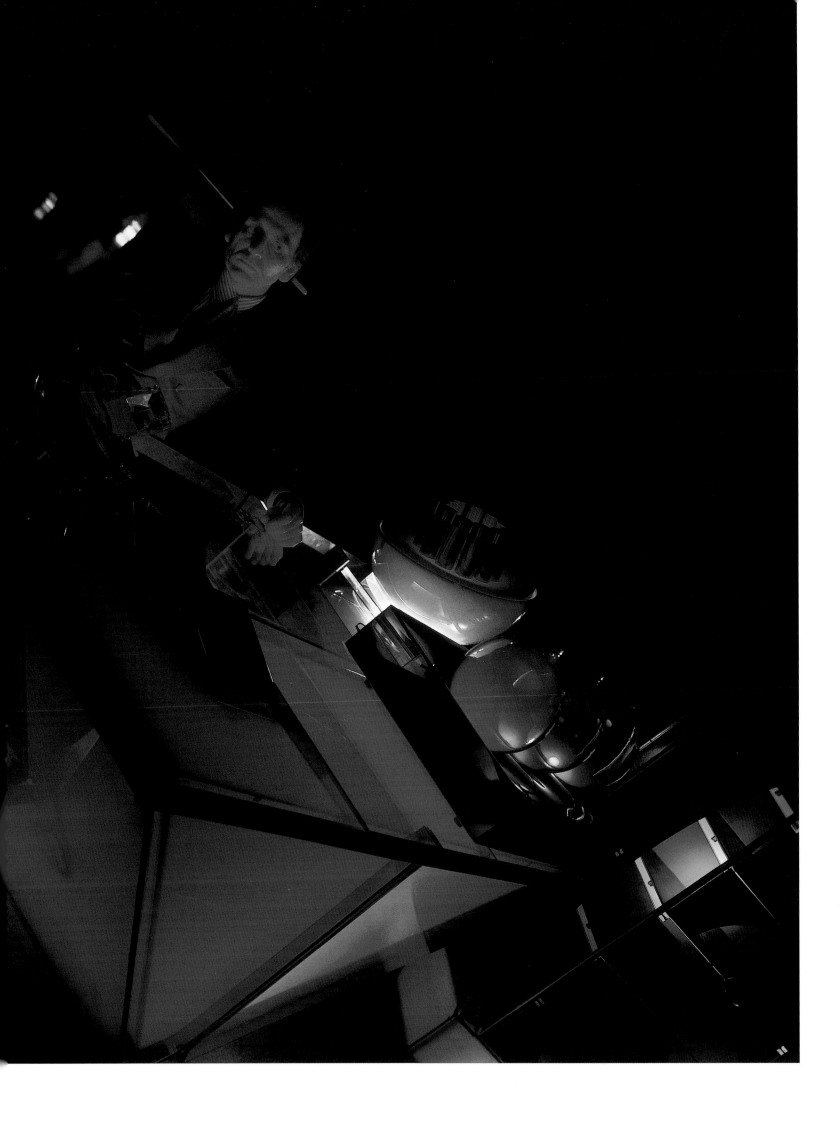

French Design

French furniture is showcased every year at the Paris trade fairs. The Société des Artistes Décorateurs (SAD) comprises artists working in fields as diverse as architecture, interior design, furniture, mural art, textiles, wallpaper, etc. Its mission was to promote creativity and, in the 1960s, the SAD was a breeding ground for fledgling designers. Within this association rooted in a sense of tradition and expertise, the notion of the decorator was still very much alive. The definition offered by master glassmaker André-Louis Pierre, by way of introduction to the Salon des Artistes Décorateurs in 1961, remains close to the one that had evolved in the 1950s: a "collaborator with the architect, adviser to the user, and project manager." Against this dull backdrop, one man, François Mathey, attempted to awaken minds to and focus energies on the existence of the object. In 1962, with the help of Yolande Amic, he staged an exhibition, *Antagonism 2—the Object*, at the Musée des Arts Décoratifs in Paris that amounted to a declaration of intent.

Sculptors and painters were invited to help to contribute to a fresh understanding of the art of living that would signal a complete break with the trend of industrial aesthetics. François Mathey wrote, "So it was that the object might be considered outside the universally accepted industrial, decorative, or functional norms; artists might realize that the humdrum, everyday, external world was also of concern to them, also belonged to them, and that they had a right, a duty to baptize it."

There was no lack of designers in France. However, still attached to their traditions, they tended to subscribe to the well-groomed elegance extolled by the Scandinavians and shared their conception of modernity. The younger generation was looking for heroes, but, despite the efforts of institutions, such as the Union Centrale des Arts Décoratifs, the SAD, the UAM, and *Formes Utiles*, and the success of the many exhibitions, there was little impact on the French public before the end of the decade, with the 1968 exhibition *Domus, Formes Italiens*, organized by Marc Berthier at Galeries Lafayette in Paris.

Paradoxically, in 1960, when the Thirty-first Salon des Arts Ménagers opened its 96,000 square yards (80,000

Facing page: Office of the couturier Pierre Cardin. Photo: Carol Marc Lavrillier.

Christian Daninos, chair, 1968. Polyester shell, steel and cloth. Courtesy Drouot-Presse, Paris. © Adagp, Paris 2003.

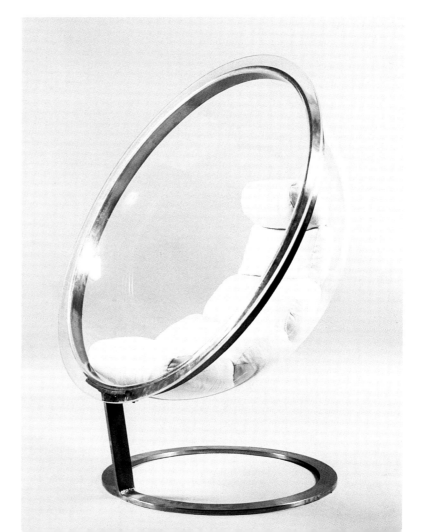

square meters) in the Centre National des Industries et des Techniques (CNIT) at La Défense just outside Paris, visitors arrived in droves, 1,426,533 to be exact. In the giddy atmosphere of this highly popular show, it was the domestic gadgetry that attracted visitors, while the *Foyer d'aujourd'hui* section

displayed projects to which the general public paid scant attention. Organized by Paul Breton, it was here that Pierre Paulin—against a very Op Art backdrop—was to exhibit his furniture produced by Artifort for the first time. "*Formes Utiles* was the exhibition one had to visit and just see the forty or so objects selected,' Michel Mortier recalled. As expertise without exposure is destined to remain unrecognized, it was lucky that the careers of the young designers at the time were promoted by the magazine *Maison française*. Solange Gorse, the magazine's editor-in-chief since 1946, was a woman with an eye for talent and future trends.

**Charles Zublena,
wooden recliner.
Courtesy Galerie Jousse
Entreprise, Paris.
Photo: Marc Domage.**

Bernard Govin,
reclining sofa in
modular elements, 1967.
Photo: Pierre Joly
and Véra Cardot.
© Adagp, Paris 2003.

In 1964, under the aegis of the Mobilier National—France's stock of state-owned furniture—and at the initiative of Culture Minister André Malraux, the Atelier de Recherche et de Création (ARC) was created. Set up by Jean Coural, this promotional organization was intended to further the advances in innovation and research being made by French interior design that were split between logical, modernist developments emerging from the tradition of the Union des Artistes Modernes (UAM) and Functionalism, and more forward-thinking initiatives based on the implementation of recent materials and techniques.

Bernard Quentin, furniture in
structured "honeycomb"
cardboard, 1967.
Courtesy Bernard Quentin.
© Adagp, Paris 2003.

Facing page: Bernard Quentin,
armchair in the form of a
truncated cylinder, c. 1967.
Courtesy Bernard Quentin.
© Adagp, Paris 2003.

The founder's goal was to encourage the many designers and other visual artists to return the Mobilier National to its glory, when a sovereign might regularly refurbish his residences and thus knowingly give impetus to the decorative arts in the process. The ARC made it possible for the French government to reestablish its links with tradition by placing at the disposal of designers the complex tools that would allow them to tackle contemporary manufacturing, thus compensating for a furniture industry that had remained slower than those of other countries (Italy in particular) to capitalize on new technologies. One of the ARC's first decisions was to dispatch Roger Legrand's Pan-U system to the Thirteenth Milan Triennale. The system and a theater seat carried off prizes, while the French section saw itself awarded the Triennale's grand prix. Early efforts (Philippon-Lecoq, Guy Duval, Joseph-André Motte, Michel Boyer) were still under the influence of the modern movement. The push for innovation was spurred by collaboration with Olivier Mourgue, in charge of the designs for the furniture in the French pavilion at the Montreal World's Fair in 1967.

It fell to Pierre Paulin to curate the space in the French pavilion at the 1970 World's Fair in Osaka. Paulin's own creations were presented, notably the Boudin tricolore, as was Roger Tallon's Cryptogamme. After 1967, the ARC also participated in the Salon des Artistes Décorateurs and the organization soon took on responsibility for other collective events. For a 1968 design for the Maison de la Culture in Rennes, Olivier Mourgue contributed the cafeteria, Pierre Paulin the book and recordings libraries, while the lobby was the fruit of a collaborative effort. In the same year, Édouard Albert fitted out the library at Nanterre. For his part, Alain Richard focused his studies on clinical equipment, designing a hospital bed. The architects Jouven and Phelouzat devised a partition capable of bearing both bathroom facilities and lighting. Joseph Motte came up with the offices for the prefect and for the chairman of the council for the new prefecture at Cergy. As for Pierre Guariche, he designed the office of the prefect at Évry. Feasibility studies were also undertaken: Olivier Mourgue tackled transformable housing, fitting out an 860-square-foot (eighty-square-meter) apartment with kitchen and bathroom units, incorporating mobile rooms and partitions.

By the time of the French pavilion at the 1968 Milan Triennale, François Mathey could thus sum up French design: "Since they are in fact pilot projects, some French initiatives are likely to solicit large-scale competitions: such is the case with state initiatives, for example, through the creative studio arm of the Mobilier National that give artists an opportunity to study prototypes; so, too, any department store keen to distribute products that fulfil precise quality and price criteria." It is intriguing to note that this way of thinking about the manufactured object seeks to preserve many of the qualities of unity implicit in the work of art. Perhaps it was to France's benefit that it did not dispose of a manufacturing and distribution infrastructure able to create beauty of a rational, absolute, conventional, and convenient type.

In a remark that highlights a central feature of the *exception française*, François Mathey wrote: "Among everything arising from our environment that in consequence aids us in organizing interior and exterior space visually, the French section's concern has been to select works of indisputable aesthetic quality designed industrially and mass-produced, or potentially so ... The idea that the beautiful is synonymous with the expensive, that quality is the prerogative of one-shot objects, is no more than a lovingly tended illusion" (Introductory text to the catalog for the French section at the Fourteenth Milan Triennale in 1968).

In the wake of the vogue for the Scandinavian approach and for the purism of the straight line, however, a more flexible way of thinking gained ground, corresponding to a sense of release, to a shift in attitude. In 1968, Mathey, then head conservator at the Musée des Arts Décoratifs, appointed Yolande Amic and Yvonne Brunhammer curators of a major exhibition on the modern chair, *Les Assises du Siège Contemporain*, an overview of seating design that heralded a new level of awareness in France. In her foreword, Yolande Amic declared, "Inventiveness has never, at any time, been wanting in France ... Among the young, two names predominate, Paulin and Mourgue, one manufactured in Holland by Artifort, the other in France by Airborne.

Pierre Paulin, Ribbon Chair,
model 582, 1965.
Tubular frame with
foam padding,
Larsen fabric covers.
Photo: Carol Marc Lavrillier

They were the first to make seating
without apparent structure in polyester
foam over a tubular metal framework,
creating colorful, organic, and absolutely
original forms." This initial recognition
was also the act that laid the
foundations of contemporary design.

Pierre Paulin (1927–). Receptive to color
and form as a result of studying
ceramics and sculpture, Paulin entered
Maxime Old's workshop at the École
Camondo where he obtained
a grounding in tradition as well as
in modernity. Early on, he became
interested in seating and collaborated
with the Thonet company, where he
learned to tackle new materials such as
molded plywood, reinforced polyester,
and foam rubber. After 1958, he joined
the design office of Dutch firm Artifort.

Paulin was technically gifted, and
in 1959–60 his investigations led to
the production of the 560 armchair,
whose structure is covered in foam,
with a flexible, elastic jersey cover,
encasing both the organic-looking chair
and its toadstool-shaped footrest.
For the 1966 Ribbon chair, he worked as
a sculptor, shaping latex foam attached
to a light tubular metal frame. His
investigations into form continued with
the Tongue chair of 1967. Functional
seating of this kind was a formal
statement of the spirit of the 1960s.
The first to introduce curves into
furniture, Paulin, contrary to the tenets
of industrial design, concealed the
structure. As a forerunner of the hippie
culture, with the Tapis Séjour created
in 1965 and manufactured by Roche-
Bobois, he promoted a new, floor-level

lifestyle. He proclaimed this desire for freedom through understated, poetic works. In 1968, the Mobilier International company brought out the Déclive seat, an offshoot of his earlier Tapis Séjour. The same year, he was commissioned to change the lighting and furnishings in the Grande Galerie in the Louvre. His designs, including circular foam benches, marked the onset of his collaboration with the Mobilier National. Jean Coural, director of the Mobilier National, then commissioned work from Paulin for

Above: Pierre Paulin,
Tulip swivel chair, 1962.
Shell-shape seat,
foam padding, fabric
cover, on steel base.
Artifort, Schijndel.
Courtesy Galerie
de Casson Méron, Paris.

Below: Pierre Paulin,
Tulip 545 armchairs, 1965.
Artifort, Schijndel.
Courtesy Artifort, Schijndel.
Photo: Paul Genest.

approach was sometimes misunderstood by his contemporaries, he was still a pioneer in the introduction of inflatable furniture (1961). Panton's first chair, the Cone chair, is still his most famous, its form constituting not an end in itself but a means to an end. In 1960, for the restaurant in the Astoria Hotel at Trondheim, Panton conceived a total environment, extending over the entire room from wall to ceiling, that employed patterns derived from Op Art and abolished all internal spatial divisions. This innovative path was to find complete expression in 1970 in the now legendary Visiona 2 interior commissioned by Bayer and exhibited in Cologne. The culmination was the organic interior of the Phantasy Landscape. Panton was destined to walk this new creative path alone, with only Pierre Paulin and Joe Colombo daring to offer solutions that were as radical.

Color is one of the key elements of Panton's work ("color is more significant than form"), and it is color that confers the spirit of the space. In 1963, Panton moved on, establishing an agency in Basel. One design dating from 1959–60, the stackable Panton chair made of a single stretch of molded plastic, was a superb creation; it was to be produced by Herman Miller in 1967. In 1960, Verner Panton came up with the Modular chair, constructed out of chromium-plated metal with circular foam-rubber cushions. In 1962, he designed the free forms of a mobile seating concept, the Caster Easy chair, followed by the Flying chair that spreads into all three dimensions in 1963. The 1969 Living Tower, a structure comprising a wooden frame upholstered in foam and wrapped in elastic covers, offered seating on four levels, like a room within a room.

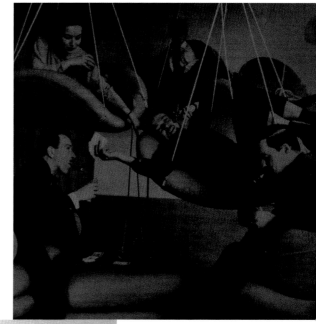

Verner Panton, suspended Flying chairs, 1963–64. Courtesy Verner Panton Design, Basel.

Verner Panton, upholstered chair, metal frame on casters, latex foam padding, fabric cover, 1963. Storz + Palmer.

Poul M. Volther,
Corona chair,
model EJ 5, 1960.
Chromium-plated
structure, fabric-covered
foam padding.
Erik Jorgensen Möbelfabrik.
Courtesy Erik Jorgensen
Möbelfabrik, Denmark.

Facing page: Yrjö
Kukkapuro, 412 armchair,
1964.
Fiberglass shell seat
on a steel base.
Avarte Oy, Helsinki.
Courtesy Avarte Oy, Helsinki.

Eero Aarnio (1932–). After studying at the School of Applied Art in Helsinki, Aarnio worked for the furniture manufacturer Asko from 1960 to 1962, before founding his own studio in 1962. An independent artist-decorator, Aarnio also designed furniture. Starting in the 1960s, however, his abiding interest became plastics, and he edged towards a more "space age" type of design. He created the Globe armchair, which offered an integrated environment with extras such as a telephone and a stereo (1963), the Gyro chair (1967–68), and the Pastilli easy chair (1967). In 1965, he won first prize with a series of storage pieces and chairs at the international competition in Cantù, Italy.

Nanna Ditzel (1923–). She began training as a cabinetmaker before embarking on studies at the School of Arts and Crafts and the Royal Academy of Fine Art in Copenhagen. It was not long (1946) before she opened a design office with Jorgen Ditzel. From the very start of her career, she embraced the challenge presented by new materials and techniques. In the 1950s, she addressed a new concept in living space with a selection of multi-level benches. In 1962, she produced the Sun Trap, an outdoor furniture unit in the form of an enclosed space made of timber and equipped with cushions that could accommodate up to fourteen people. In 1963, she created wooden playground equipment for children. In 1965, she developed furniture using foam rubber, including a set of cushions upholstered in brightly colored knitted fabric, whose shapes can be varied, combined, and arranged into a congenial living space.

New British Design

Roger Dean, Sea Urchin chair, 1968. Hille, London. Courtesy Hille, London.

With Mary Quant's miniskirt, music by *The Beatles* and *The Rolling Stones*, Pop Art and fashion (the first Mr. Freedom store opened in 1969), Swinging was at the cutting edge of youth lifestyle. Pop culture was extremely lively in Britain as a whole from the beginning of the 1960s, thanks in part to the efforts of a progressive group of artists and critics who had emerged in the previous decade, the Independent Group (formed in 1952). With the aim of understanding technical advances in American industry and alive to the telltale signs of what was to become pop culture, in 1956 the group (including Richard Hamilton, Eduardo Paolozzi, Reyner Banham, and Peter and Alison Smithson) organized an exhibition, *The House of the Future*, which contained the seeds of a new English furniture style. Eschewing

Alan Turville, Kompass 1 table, 1968.
Melamine top.
Hille, London.
Courtesy Design Council Slide
Collection at Manchester
Metropolitan University, Manchester.
© Design Council.

Executive desk with frame in
perforated smoked Plexiglas.

the modernist approach, Hamilton famously identified the characteristics of Pop Art as "popular, transient, expendable, low-cost, mass-produced, young, witty, sexy, glamorous, and big business." "Popular" art was elevated to the level of art proper by the Independent Group, and they embarked on a long series of lectures and seminars. Yet at this time British furniture—painted wood, brightly colored inflatable or plastic elements, kits, painted plywood—left no lasting mark on design history. If ideas—often eccentric—abounded, they were conveyed through the accumulation of objects and gadgets without rhyme or reason. Modular furniture was all

the rage. In 1967, the Design Centre hosted an exhibition, *Prototype Furniture*, which showed Roger Dean's polyurethane foam Sea Urchin manufactured by Hille (1968) and David Goodship's double rocking chair. Creations like these were promoted by magazines, such as the weekend supplement to the *Times* and *Nova*. In February 1962, the *Sunday Times* was the first to devote a supplement ("Design for Living") to this new lifestyle. Response was mixed: at that time, the general public, starved of ornament since the Utility Furniture of the war years, was intent on a return to color and, especially, to a wider range of choice.

Peter Murdoch, disposable child's chair, 1964–65. Polyethylene-coated cardboard.
Peter Murdoch Inc.
Courtesy Victoria & Albert Museum, London.
© V&A Images.

Jean Schofield and Walker Wright Schofield, mobile compact Capsule kitchen, incorporating oven, refrigerator, storage units, and work surface, 1968.
Courtesy Design Council Slide Collection at Manchester Metropolitan University, Manchester.
© Design Council.

Peter Murdoch (1940–). In 1963, Murdoch designed a child's chair made out of cardboard decorated with a typically Pop Art color pattern. This innovative piece was built from a single sheet of plastic-coated cardboard and sold in a flat pack. Soon joined by other works (a chair and a table) produced in accordance with similar principles, the chair was developed for mass consumption at a rock-bottom price. It nonetheless remains a watershed image of the 1960s and won a Design Award.

Bernard Holdaway. In 1966, Holdaway designed a novel furniture range dubbed the Tom o'Tom with varnished cardboard table and chairs based on the circle and produced by Hull Traders Furniture. Throwaway paper furniture was one of the hallmarks of consumer society; like Murdoch, Holdaway believed that a furniture designer should not take himself too seriously.

Max Clendinning designed furniture constructed from twenty-five plywood elements that could be combined in a hundred variations: chairs, sofas, tables, and storage units. Though relatively expensive, this "transformable furniture" met with incredible success, owing precisely to its capacity to evolve. Collapsible, foldaway furniture was very much in vogue during the 1960s: customers liked to take away kits and assemble the elements at home. In this way, the Habitat principle— in-store design freely available to the customer—came into being.

des Arts Ménagers, with its *Foyer d'aujourd'hui* section. These exhibitions also served as a platform where designers could make contacts with business (Glaces de Boussois, Formica, Saint-Gobain, etc.). Ever responsive to life and to those around him, Jacques Dumond's philosophy was, "To learn to make the most out of the legacies of the past and the discoveries of the present . . . basically, for me, the main thing is to be alive among the living" (P. Renous, *Portraits de décorateurs*, 1969). Dumond passed on not only his knowledge of furniture, but also the importance of understanding the client

and the system of design production. It was under him that Janine Abraham and Dirk Jan Rol both trained.

Marcel Gascoin preached a functional solution for each specific case: "The case is the conjunction 'apartment plus occupant'; the apartment is defined by its layout and by the elements provided for comfort. The occupant is defined by his family makeup and by his professional and social attributes" (Renous, *op. cit.*). Pierre Guariche, Michel Mortier, Joseph-André Motte, and Pierre Paulin all trained under him. Maxime Old was professor of contemporary decorative art at the Art et Technique

Claude Parent, apartment interior, Neuilly. Photo: Gilles Ehrmann.

House, Bordeaux. Split-level
living space, c. 1969.
Photo: Pascal Hinous.

Facing page: Henry Massonet,
stackable, plastic stool
that can be dismantled,
c. 1968.

center. Old possessed an insight into both: he could draw to express his ideas and ran a workshop to produce them. The last real *décorateur*, he exerted considerable influence on Pierre Paulin, among others.

René-Jean Caillette (1919–). As soon as Caillette left the École des Arts Appliqués, he became interested in mass-producing furniture. He initially spent a few years designing for Schmidt & Cie., an interior design firm in Paris's Faubourg Saint-Antoine. He steered clear of the "René Gabriel-Gascoin" school, and, with some other young designers, including Landault, set up the Groupe Saint-Honoré, which both designed and exhibited mass-produced furniture, and was supported by the magazine *Meubles et Décor*. Caillette eventually met Marcel Gascoin and became part of his circle. He exhibited regularly at the Salon des Arts Ménagers and at the Salon des Artistes Décorateurs. Plain and rigorous in style, his furniture was first produced by

Charron and then by Steiner. Around 1964, he came up with a furniture and shelving range based on a system using U-shaped pieces in materials such as steel, stainless steel, and leather. Though this was by no means his principal activity, he did tackle interior refits. An interior design consultant, he also designed the music space at the Paris headquarters of French state radio, the Maison de la Radio, in 1963.

René-Jean Caillette, shelving system exhibited at the Salon des Artistes Décorateurs, 1964.

Below: René-Jean Caillette, melamine dining-room and living-room units exhibited in 1964.

Facing page, top: Pierre Guariche, furniture exhibited at the Salon des Artistes Décorateurs in 1963. Photo: Paul Genest.

Facing page, bottom: Antoine Philippon, Jacqueline Lecoq, television and stereo bar unit, 1966. Colored melamine with stainless-steel base. Photo: Horak.

Pierre Guariche (1926–1995). After training in the decorative arts, Guariche worked for a couple of years with Marcel Gascoin, who introduced him to Michel Mortier. He exhibited at the Salon des Artistes Décorateurs and the Salon des Arts Ménagers where he obtained a measure of financial success. He then launched out on his own. Galerie Mai was the first to bring out his models, followed by Airborne and Steiner. As orders flooded in, he joined forces with Michel Mortier and Joseph-André Motte to set up the Atelier de Recherches Plastiques (ARP) group, which operated 1948 to 1951. He made a name for himself with his daybed the Vallée Blanche, produced by Huchers Minvielle in 1960. He exhibited many collections at the Salons des Arts Ménagers, elegant pieces in which color and materials both play major roles. With considerable foresight, he believed in the importance of setting up a federation for the profession, and helped the Société des Artistes Décorateurs encourage young designers to seize any chance to exhibit their work as soon as they could. In 1968,

Pierre Guariche, La Vallée
Blanche daybed, 1963.
Tubular structure, foam
padding, jersey cover.
Salon des Arts Ménagers.
Les Huchers-Minvielle.

Claude Courtecuisse,
Kenya chair, 1967.
Metal tubing, canvas,
and leather.
Steiner.
Courtesy Claude
Courtecuisse.

Facing page: Marc Held's
house in Corrèze.
Photo: Pascal Hinous.

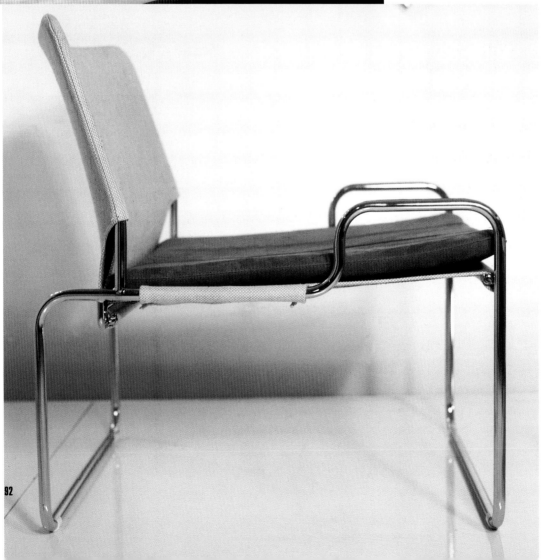

Geoffrey Harcourt,
leather bucket-chair,
chromed-metal plate base.
Artifort, 1963.

Bonet-Ferrari-Handy-
Kurchan, A.A.A. chairs.
Airborne.

Pascal Mourgue, "Papillon"
stacking chair, 1969.
Abet print, canvas seat.
Groupe Essai.

Banque Rothschild, Paris,
interior by Michel Boyer, 1970.
Stainless-steel reception desk.
Photo: Pascal Hinous.

Michel Boyer, Banque Rothschild
staff cafeteria, 1970.
Courtesy Jousse
Entreprise/Galerie de Casson,
Paris.

Michel Boyer, coffee table, 1968.
With magazine rack in white
melamine, Obeflex ash.
Courtesy Jousse Entreprise/
Galerie de Casson, Paris.

Facing page: Michel Boyer,
apartment, place
des Victoires, Paris.
Ceiling by Guy de
Rougemont, Paris, 1970.
Courtesy Jousse
Entreprise/Galerie
de Casson, Paris.

he created for the Atelier de Recherche et de Création (ARC) a set of chairs, including the Dagobert armchair, cast in one piece with a tubular structure held together with straps and wrapped in foam rubber with a jersey cover. In 1969, he produced an executive desk and an office chair in fulfillment of an order placed in 1967 and 1968 by the Mobilier National for the prefecture at Évry.

Joseph-André Motte (1925–). An architect-decorator who trained under Marcel Gascoin, from 1948 to 1951, Motte was part of the Atelier de Recherches Plastiques (ARP) adventure, before going on to obtain several commissions, including refits at Orly Airport, the harbor and administration center at Le Havre, and an air terminal at Roissy. He assisted on the restoration work on the Grande Galerie of the Louvre, designed furniture for executive offices in various prefectures at the request of the Mobilier National, and provided many private companies with models for mass production. Although they employed contemporary techniques and materials, his elegant, modern pieces eschewed ostentation. In the furniture for a girl's

bedroom presented in 1961, he used plywood and Formica, while for the Orly-Sud air terminal he combined modular seating in tubular metal and foam rubber. He preferred materials such as wood, wool, stone, leather, and glass. Avoiding gaudy color, Motte preferred materials to keep their natural hue. He particularly admired Mies van der Rohe, Aalto, and Saarinen, architects-interior designers who combined an awareness of human needs with a concern for the

lived environment, to the extent of designing everything themselves—from the cutlery to the table, chairs, rooms, and entire house. Motte's goal was to offer users spacious, functional, well-lit areas with built-in storage that would guarantee comfort and rationality, while the furniture, easily moved, would provide sufficient leeway for individual expression. Briefs for interiors for prefectures in the new towns were supported by the Atelier de Recherche et

Joseph-André Motte, stainless-steel mosaic wall decoration, 1967. Salon des Artistes Décorateurs.

Michel Mortier, split-level lounge, c. 1969.

Facing page: House, interior by David Hicks, 1969. Elda easy chair by Joe Colombo, storage units CEI Raymond Loewy. Photo: Pascal Hinous.

de Création (ARC). For Évry, Motte opted for a collection of desks in steel, Macassar ebony, and reversed leather, with desks for executives, section mangers, typists, and reception areas, as well as a hexagonal table and office armchairs.

Michel Mortier (1925–). A graduate of the École des Arts Appliqués, for four years he worked with Étienne-Henri Martin in the Studium Louvre before moving to Brussels. He became head of Marcel Gascoin's atelier, where

he remained four years. Mortier, too, was a defender of Functionalism and Rationalism. For Éditions Minvielle, he designed combination furniture before joining Guariche and Motte with whom he set up the Atelier de Recherches Plastiques (ARP), the name being chosen to appear first in the alphabetical directory. This euphoric period was to last four years. Splitting accounts and sites between them, the group brought many projects to fruition. Indeed its members proved complementary: Motte was

a tireless worker, while Guariche would attend the exhibitions and openings, and deal with client PR. The association ended rather abruptly. Mortier established his own practice in 1957 and made contacts abroad. After exhibiting the SF103 chair at the Milan Triennale in 1963, he left France to settle in Canada for a time where he was responsible for preparations for the World's Fair in Montreal. After returning to Paris in 1965, he joined as a consultant for an interior design store, the Maison Française. As customers would often

Maison de la Culture, Grenoble, built by André Wogenscky, 1967. Theater lobby with untreated concrete beams. Photo: Pascal Hinous.

Maison de la Culture, Grenoble. Central staircase with steel angle brackets. Photo: Pascal Hinous.

Alain Richard and
André Monpoix,
telephone station for
the Maison de la Culture,
Grenoble, 1967.
Red ABS shells.
Photo: Pascal Hinous.

request advice and plans, Mortier became involved in interior design. Working a great deal for private customers in this area, he remained faithful to Functionalist ideas.

Alain Richard (1926–). After attending the École des Arts Décoratifs in the workshop of René Gabriel, in 1949, Richard was then employed by the latter, who died the following year. Alain Richard then had several internships in the Netherlands. In 1952, he set up his own agency, tackling "problems dealing with the environment." He considered color very important and was helped in this area by his wife, Jacqueline Iribe, a specialist in tapestry and printed textile design. Though rooted in the classical tradition, Richard's restrained way

of thinking was nonetheless utterly contemporary. In 1967, the Atelier de Recherche et de Création (ARC) commissioned a study from him on "luxuriously comfortable [seating] for reception rooms." The units proposed— including benches, a trolley with drawers, an end table on casters, a coffee table, and an occasional table with a cigar box—were designed bottom-up from a single element: an aluminum plate of variable size in the form of an upside-down "U." Richard was once again commissioned to design seating for public areas. He designed the Coquille seat, manufactured in 1969 in white molded polyester and foam covered in orange jersey. Mortier also fitted out many banks, conference rooms, and the train stations Auber and La Défense, Paris.

Andre Monpoix (1925–1976). Monpoix trained at the École des Arts Décoratifs in ateliers headed by Rene Gabriel, Maxime Old, and finally Jacques Dumond, who between them provided him with a thorough and complementary grounding in design. Monpoix worked with Dumond for four years before showing his own furniture at exhibitions at the Salon des Arts Ménagers. He designed a series of chairs with tubular metal and plastic wire frames that were manufactured by Meubles TV. In 1967, he and Alain Richard designed a phone shell made of red ABS for a cultural center in Grenoble. In the same year, he filled an order from the Atelier de Recherche et de Création (ARC) for pieces (seats, an ottoman, and a side table with drawers) in white lacquered molded wood, a concept in "floor-level living" aimed at a younger clientele. Influenced by the Finns—he much admired how contemporary Finnish design never lost touch with its traditional roots—Monpoix's pieces are clean-lined and demonstrated a poetic awareness of form and volume.

Janine Abraham (1929–) and **Dirk Jan Rol** (1929–). Janine Abraham studied at the École des Beaux-Arts, then at the École Camondo. Dirk Jan Rol trained as a cabinetmaker in the Netherlands before coming to Paris where he took a six-month evening course at the École des Arts Appliqués, then was admitted to the École des Arts Décoratifs. His head of atelier was Louis Sognot

House, interior by Stefanidis, hall decorated with lacquer paint, 1970.
Photo: Pascal Hinous.

House, interior by Stefanidis, open-plan dining room, carpet with a large abstract pattern, 1970.
Photo: Pascal Hinous.

Facing page: House, interior by Stefanidis, 1970. Large bronze by the sculptor Rouillet. Sofa, Meuble International.
Photo: Pascal Hinous.

House built by Claude
Parent. Living room and
dining room with large
windows, 1970.
Photo: Pascal Hinous.

Facing page, top: Pierre
Gautier-Delaye, Air France
office, Cannes, 1966.
Photo: DG, Cannes.

Facing page, bottom:
Jacques Borel highway café,
interior by Pierre Gautier-
Delaye, c. 1970.

and his director Pierre Dumond. He then
worked for as a draftsman at Dumond's
where he met Janine Abraham, who
had already been working there for
a year. Abraham had attended the École
Camondo, studying with Maxime Old
who taught modernism at a time when
the "style" embodied by Jansen was
predominant. There, she saw the work
of Pierre Paulin, two years her senior,
which was a revelation for her. They
decided to leave Dumond and open an
agency in Sèvres. Like Paulin, Monpoix,
Richard, and Simard, Janine Abraham
began working for Meubles TV, a
company founded by a journalist, Lucien
Veillon, who wanted to set up a "French
Knoll." Abraham's nickname at the time
translates as "Miss Rattan," and she
exhibited her work on the stands of an
organization promoting the material.

Brought out by Rougié, the furniture
was distributed through Roche-Bobois.
Lucien Veillon then left Meubles TV for
Minvielle, an innovative company with
a foothold in various department stores
that went on to launch a score
of outlets in its own name (with two
in Paris: on the Left Bank at 17, rue du
Vieux-Colombier and on the Right Bank
at 40, rue de Châteaudun). Minvielle
was the first European producer
of modular furniture. "With my units,"
Charles Minvielle explained, "I wanted
to create a contemporary furniture style.
To do so, I had to forge an entirely
original aesthetic formula."
The furniture by Minvielle's design
team was derived from the Modulor,
brainchild of the great architect
Le Corbusier. The brilliant team
of designers the Huchers Minvielle
assembled was trained by Dirk Jan Rol,
Guariche, Mortier, Motte, Blondeau, and
Abraham. Dirk Jan Rol was then working
for Minvielle, crisscrossing France
setting up retail outlets. His chairs were
built in partnership with the Huchers,
Steiner, and Bois Béarnais Fabricants.
Veillon was sales manager, but first and
foremost he remained a journalist.
In spite of this entrepreneurial spirit,
Minvielle had arrived too late. The
Atelier de Recherches Plastiques (ARP)
and Paulin already had a toehold in the
market: Minvielle filed for bankruptcy.
A visit by a group of nine store owners
to Ikea provided food for thought; from
their subsequent decision to join forces,
was born Conforama, which occupied
Dirk Jan Rol for many years. As an
architect, he designed fifteen of the
company's outlets. Having constructed

the first in the Landes region with Roger Taillibert, he went on to plan and build one on his own at Sèvres.

Pierre Gautier-Delaye (1923–). Gautier-Delaye trained at the École des Arts Décoratifs under its open-minded director, Leon Moussinac. Heads of atelier included Étienne-Henri Martin, Rene Gabriel, and Louis Sognot. His studies completed, he entered the practice of architect Henri-Jacques Lemême. Taking his cue from Savoyard architecture, Lemême, an excellent teacher who had worked under Laprade, impressed upon Gautier-Delaye the need to be honest with materials. He instilled him with a love of wood and high-quality raw materials. Paul Breton, director of the Salon des Arts Ménagers and of the "Foyer d'aujourd'hui" section, then invited young designers to present models for the annual exhibition: entries deemed acceptable would be manufactured. Thanks to Breton, Gautier-Delaye was able to set up his first stand and present a suite called Week-end, made of pine from the Landes, that met with great success: it was brought out by Vergneres. Gautier-Delaye worked part-time for an American, Harold Bennett, who opened an agency, the Paris branch of Raymond Loewy's New York-based office, the Compagnie d'Esthétique Industrielle (CEI). A French-born naturalized American, Loewy wanted to set up in France. Gautier-Delaye worked as director of the agency for seven years; Loewy taught him both the trade and a feeling for business. The New York agency enlisted the services of two

hundred draftsmen. The Paris office numbered about thirty employees divided into three sectors: design, graphic design, and interior design. Gautier-Delaye oversaw the interior design department. Customers included department store BHV, Puy city council, and Air France. One Air France contract slipped through the fingers of the CEI agency, and Gautier-Delaye eventually handled it himself. He then opened his own

agency and designed interiors for seventy-seven Air France agencies throughout the world. He was also behind a number of Jacques Borel's hotels and highway restaurants, and fitted out Paris metro stations, including La Défense and Kléber. He also worked for the construction workers' national pension fund. Later in his career his focus was almost exclusively on interior design.

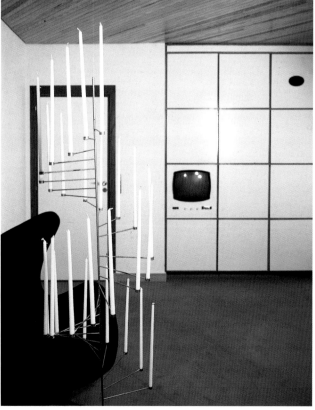

Apartment and furniture
by Marc Held, 1965.
Candlestick by
Poul Kjaerholm.
Photo: Pascal Hinous.

Facing page: Moulin
des Corbeaux, property
decorated by Charles
Sévigny, 1966.
Photo: Pascal Hinous.

the number of designers on its books, including Marcel Breuer and Sebastiano Matta.

Eero Saarinen (1910–1961). Having immigrated to the United States in 1923, Saarinen studied under his father and designed furniture for him from 1929 to 1933. He then spent two years in Paris during which he studied sculpture at the Académie de la Grande Chaumière. After his return to the United States, he met Charles Eames. Their collaboration proved short-lived, however, as Saarinen felt a growing concern with the concept and approached furniture as sculpture. He took part in the *Organic Design in Home Furnishing* competition. He met Florence Knoll and, in 1943, created his first wooden molded chair for Knoll. Other models in molded fiberglass followed in 1946, then came the Womb chair, produced in 1948, and some time later the Pedestal and Chair group, produced in 1955–56. This collection, with its one-piece aluminum bases and

molded plastic seats, was a remarkable feat. In 1950, he established his own office at Bloomfield Hills. He designed the TWA Terminal at New York's John F. Kennedy Airport (1956–1962) and the CBS offices in the same city (1960–64). In 1961, Saarinen died, aged only 51, in an accident.

Warren Platner (1919–). An architect by training, Platner worked for Raymond Loewy and the architects Peï and Roche & Dinkeloo from 1945 to 1950. He was then

Richard Schultz,
Outdoor dining furniture,
adjustable sun bed
and occasional table, 1966.
© Richard Schultz.

Charles Eames, Tandem
Sling Seating, public
amenity series, 1965.
Courtesy Herman Miller,
Zeeland.
Photo: Charles Eames.

associated with Eero Saarinen's company as architect-designer, finally setting up his own architecture practice in New York in 1965. Between 1963 and 1967, Warren Platner collaborated with Knoll's development division, a joint venture that led to one of his most widely admired creations, the Wire Based Group, a collection of tables, stools, and chairs based on nickel-plated steel whose visual effect is evocative of Kinetic Art. Warren Platner was a great admirer of the work of sculptor Naum Gabo.

Bill Stephens. Stephens was educated at Philadelphia's College of Art, and his investigations centered on the chair. His career testifies to a fruitful combination of method, coupled with the use of classic and recent materials. For Knoll he made an original yet comfortable collection of molded plywood seats. Though discreet, the effect was superb (1967–71).

Harry Bertoia (1915–1978). Having studied at both Cass Technical High School and later at the Detroit Society of Arts and Crafts, Bertoia benefited from training on two fronts. In 1943, he left Michigan and joined Charles and Ray Eames in California, where he focused primarily on metalwork, whereas the Eames wanted to pursue investigations into wood. They parted ways and in 1946 Bertoia started working for Knoll Associates. His finest models, such as the Diamond and Bird chairs, saw

Facing page: Offices designed by interior decorator Noël Davoine, 1971. The lobby is treated in granite; the Wire Group chairs are by Warren Platner. Photo: Pascal Hinous.

Charles Eames, Time-Life office armchairs, 1960. Steel and leather. Courtesy Herman Miller, Zeeland. Photo: Earl Woods.

the light of day in the 1950s. The idea behind these pieces was based on form and space, as well as their wire frames. In 1969, Knoll changed its name to Knoll International. One of its main activities was office interiors. The models it came out with over the succeeding decades—still in production today—are now considered classics. In 1955, the company reissued creations by the trailblazer Mies van der Rohe. Knoll's policy of reissuing design was a great success in the 1960s and the following decades.

Herman Miller Inc.
Beginning in the 1930s, Herman Miller Inc. was one of the largest companies producing modern furniture in the United States. The company was managed by Dirk Jan Depree beginning in 1919. From 1947 to 1965, George Nelson, a man who understood the existing and potential demands of the high-end design market, was artistic director, and Charles Eames brought to the company his genius as a designer. The problematic of the space–work relationship was investigated further following the creation in 1960 of the Herman Miller Research Corporation,

headed by Robert Propst, which produced the Action Office and Co/Struc. To corroborate its research in this area, Herman Miller turned to ergonomic studies in the behavioral sciences. In 1962, Hugh Depree took over at the head of the company. In 1964, Propst and Nelson developed The Action Office Concept—Action Office 1, comprising independent units that can be configured into an adaptable office space. The company then underwent a period of exceptional expansion. In 1967, in Switzerland, it introduced the Panton chair in plastic molded as a single piece. Herman Miller began making inroads into the international market in 1957 with its operations in Europe, Asia, and Canada.

George Nelson (1907–). He was the first of the group (Nelson, Eames, Girard, Propst) to work for Herman Miller Inc. It was Nelson who brought in Charles Eames. Nelson was a strategist, responsible for advertising and catalogs, as well as for the company's famous logo. His architectural training led him to follow the development of that discipline. In the mid-1940s, he wrote

The Industrial Architecture of Albert Kahn and co-authored *Tomorrow's House* with Henry Wright. In 1945, he created the Storage Wall, a project publicized in *Life* magazine in conjunction with an exhibition at Macy's in New York. It presented a solution to how to store the flood of consumer durables in the modern world: a flexible wall-storage system that made for a significant saving in space. He was noticed by D. J. Depree, who in 1959 enlisted him to join the Herman Miller team. The company then manufactured the Nelson Comprehensive Storage System, the principle of which was to expand vertically and free up living space. The support consisted of a grooved strut to which all the storage compartments were attached. George Nelson wrote extensively on design, analyzing methods of product development and even producing a slide slow he later turned into a film entitled *The Civilised City*.

Charles Eames (1907–1978). In the months following his success in 1940 at the Museum of Modern Art competition dedicated to *Organic Design*, Eames

Facing page: George Nelson, combination desk with storage area and workstation; office armchair designed by Charles Eames. Herman Miller Inc., Zeeland. Courtesy Herman Miller Inc., Zeeland.

Charles Eames, stools, 1960. Walnut. Courtesy Herman Miller, Zeeland. Photo: Earl Woods.

became aware of the inadequacies of the mass-production system when applied to the furniture industry. In 1946, pursuing his interest in modes of production, he took the opportunity offered by Herman Miller Inc. to move from single objects to mass production. The advantage of molded plywood chairs is lightness and stackability. Technology advanced, and by 1950 the seats were being molded in plastic. In 1956, Eames created a superb armchair with ottoman in bent rosewood. Imposing yet comfortable, the chair was a huge hit. In 1958, the design office developed an aluminum seating range intended for outside use. In 1960, Eames came up with the Fonda chair and, in 1961, the Time-Life chair. Ongoing research led to the Evolutionary

Aluminum Group Chairs, pieces based on the principle of stretching trim and cover over an aluminum frame. A series of chairs, office chairs, tandem seats, and modular seating originated from this principle, with Tandem Sling Seating produced in 1961 for airports, the 1968 Billy Wilder chair, and the 1969 Soft Pad chair.

Alexander Girard (1907–). Brought up and educated in Florence, Girard studied architecture in London. He opened his first architectural practice in Florence before settling in New York in 1932. In 1937, he moved to Detroit with his wife. In 1943, he was hired by Ford as a designer and, two years later, became consultant colorist for General Motors. In 1952, he was hired as design director

in the textile division of Herman Miller Inc. Girard was to convey his faith in humanism through color and motifs taken from folk art and art brut. Herman Miller's catalog included ideas for color schemes by Girard adapted to interiors and exhibition halls. Girard came away from his encounter with Dorothy Liebes and Jim Thompson with a pronounced taste for vibrant colors: Mexican pinks, the scarlet of Chinatown. In 1960, his radical interior for the La Fonda del Sol Restaurant in New York was festive in spirit; designed from floor to ceiling and right down to the color of the buttons on the waiters' tunics, it captured a range of differently lit moods. This extremely modish restaurant was patronized by figures from the worlds of politics and show business. A few years later, in 1966, Girard was hired to design an interior for the Star Restaurant. Quite different in approach, elegant and discreet in its colors, it was inspired by the Art Deco style of the steamer the *Normandie*. In 1961, in order to showcase more pieces by Girard, Herman Miller opened the Textiles and Objects (T&O) store in Manhattan. Girard selected all the merchandise and exhibited all his collections there.

Robert Propst (1921–). Although Propst trained as a painter and sculptor, his furniture is not, strictly speaking, artistic. In 1964, he created the Action Office 1 Concept. This development in office furnishing arose from many preliminary studies exploring how men and women operate in the office.

The analysis of this data led to Propst's basic system. This incorporates an infinitely variable arrangement of storage units fastened to partitions or hung on the wall that can be adapted to the requirements or specifications of the office concerned. This initial effort led, in 1968, to Action Office 2. Propst eventually turned his attention to the hospital environment, designing the Pediatrics Bed in 1967, before going on in 1968 to create the Coherent Structure Hospital System (Co/Struc). Later, he developed programs for university and industry. In 1968, Propst was appointed chairman of the Herman Miller Research Corporation. His aim was to make an impact on the period with products perfectly suited to their function. Propst's output is generally neutral in color so as to maintain availability and facilitate stock management. To his mind, color is best confined to accessories, chairs for example, as they are less trouble to restyle in response to changes in taste and fashion.

Facing page: Alexander Girard, interior fitting for the La Fonda del Sol restaurant, 1960. Courtesy Herman Miller, Inc. Zeeland.

Richard Schultz, outdoor dining furniture: armchair, footstool, and coffee table, 1966. © Richard Schultz.

Charles Eames, Action
Office I, office units, 1964.
Herman Miller, Zeeland.
Courtesy Herman Miller Inc.
Zeeland.

Charles Eames, Contract
Storage S1, modular, runner-
mounted storage system,
1965. Herman Miller Inc.
Zeeland.

Facing page: Alexandre
Girard, living-room
furniture, 1967.
Courtesy Herman Miller Inc.
Zeeland.
Photo: Hm 132.

The Modern Movement in Britain

For British design, coming into being during restrictions and austerity, and attaining its high point in the 1960s, this period is a watershed. A new modernism flourished in Britain, however, thanks to the appearance of well-designed furniture in administrative offices. The status of British design on the world stage in the 1950s was largely due to figures such as Robin Day, Ernest Race, Herbert Read, and Gordon Russell, the most active players in the industry during the post-war period. In the early 1960s, the contemporary style was overwhelmed and transformed by the onslaughts of Pop Art and pop culture. Certain factors affected the world of design in general, while an anarchical spirit spread via the Pop readings of contemporary design that had begun to invade the street. The Design Centre was established in 1956 by the Council of Industrial Design in an effort to foster "good design." Accessible to the public and professionals alike, the center's official purpose betrayed a desire to guide a society in the grip of visual chaos towards the path of "good design." The council was backed in this endeavor by the Victoria & Albert Museum in London, which staged exhibitions of contemporary craft and design.

The magazine *Design*, founded in 1948, devoted page after page to these activities and kept the British public abreast of developments both at home and abroad. In national terms, Britain made its mark with a thorough analysis of the interface between creativity and function. In this reconfigured landscape, talents like John and Sylvia Reid made an impact with the elegant minimalist furniture they created

Facing page: Robin Day, MK2 stackable chair, 1963. Plastic. Hille, London. Courtesy Victoria & Albert Museum, London. © V&A Images.

Robin Day, Group Seating, 1961. Hille, London. Courtesy Hille, London.

Living-room display,
exhibited at the Council
of Industrial Design, 1963.
Courtesy Design Council
Slide Collection at
Manchester Metropolitan
University, Manchester.
© Design Council.

Robert Heritage, Britannia
and Columbia chairs
designed for the restaurant
on the steamer *Queen
Elizabeth II*, 1969.
Race Furniture Ltd.
Courtesy Design Council
Slide Collection at
Manchester Metropolitan
University, Manchester.
© Design Council.

William Plunkett, Oxted
series chair, 1965.
Courtesy Design Council
Slide Collection at
Manchester Metropolitan
University, Manchester.
© Design Council.

for Stag. Robert Heritage worked
for Archie Shine, the acme of British
refinement and functionality. Brooke
Marine, Robin Cruikshank and the
sober, subtle proportions of chairs
made by Dick Russell for Coventry
Cathedral, consecrated in 1962, attest
to considerable creative energy.
Steel began to be used for interior
design, joining natural materials, such
as wood and leather, as well as fabric
trimmings, which, occupying pride
of place in the domestic interior,
conferred warmth to what
were otherwise austere creations.

Hille From 1949, the firm of Hille began
looking to the future and to modern
furnishings with the collaboration of
Robin Day, who was to act as its
éminence grise until the 1970s. He led
the company in a direction that implied
the use of new materials and recent
manufacturing techniques. During the
1950s and 1960s, the Hille company's
modern furniture was designed
primarily by Day, but furniture to
order was also signed by other names—
Saarinen's creations for the U.S. Embassy
in London, Marcel Breuer's for the
UNESCO Headquarters in Paris, and the
furniture for the Hilton Hotel, Istanbul,

Interior of a vacation home,
exhibited at the Design
Centre, London, 1960.
Courtesy Design Council
Slide Collection at
Manchester Metropolitan
University, Manchester.
© Design Council.

Lady Margaret Casson,
dining room for
the exhibition *New
Dimension Living*, 1963.
Maple & Co.
Courtesy Design Council
Slide Collection at
Manchester Metropolitan
University, Manchester.
© Design Council.

Arne Jacobsen (1902–1971). Trained at the Royal School of Fine Art in Copenhagen, Jacobsen was an architect who produced furniture in response to construction contracts: the Novo pharmaceutical laboratory (1952), for which he designed the Ant chair; the Royal Hotel (1958), which he adorned with his Egg chair; for the City Hall at Rodovre, he proposed a variant on the Ant, the Seven (1961) conference chair. He also designed a high-back chair for Saint Catherine's College, Oxford (1962). The Danish National Bank, was furnished with a 308 chair encased in brown leather. These creations earned him the reputation of being one of the chief promulgators of Danish design.

Poul Kjaerholm (1929–1980). A cabinet-maker by training, Kjaerholm began teaching in 1952. His work is renowned for its use of matte chrome-plated steel. With their emphasis on structural elements, his pieces are close to sculpture. This is borne out in his masterpiece, the PK24 lounge chair (1965). His style claims ascendance from an international Functionalism owing much to the Bauhaus.

Den Permanente. Opening in Copenhagen in 1931, Den Permanente exhibited a selection of articles highlighting Danish craftsmanship and home design. Drawing together companies and individuals, the goal of the association was to ensure exposure for the best Danish design. The objects selected by the jury were exhibited on a permanent basis and were available for purchase. The popularity of Scandinavian design was such that Den Permanente opened an outlet in New York that was a huge success in the 1960s.

In 1955, a major exhibition held at Helsingborg in Sweden, celebrating 25 years of Functionalism, offered an overview of Swedish design and included a section devoted to the fitting of interiors for the public sector, an abiding concern in the 1960s. The show took account of such significant lifestyle changes as the use of the automobile and the introduction of the TV set,

Facing page: Mikael Bjornstjerna, molded polyurethane armchair on casters, stainless steel base. Overman.

Antti Nurmesniemi, kit armchair, c. 1960. Wood. Courtesy Studio Nurmesniemi KY, Helsinki.

Antti Nurmesniemi, chair, 1964. Steel and acrylic. Courtesy Studio Nurmesniemi KY, Helsinki.

Poul Kjaerholm, Pk-12 chair,
1964. Canework and steel.
Kold Christensen.
Courtesy Galerie Dansk
MöbelKunst, Paris.

Poul Kjaerholm, Hammock
recliner, model PK24, 1965.
Steel and rattan.

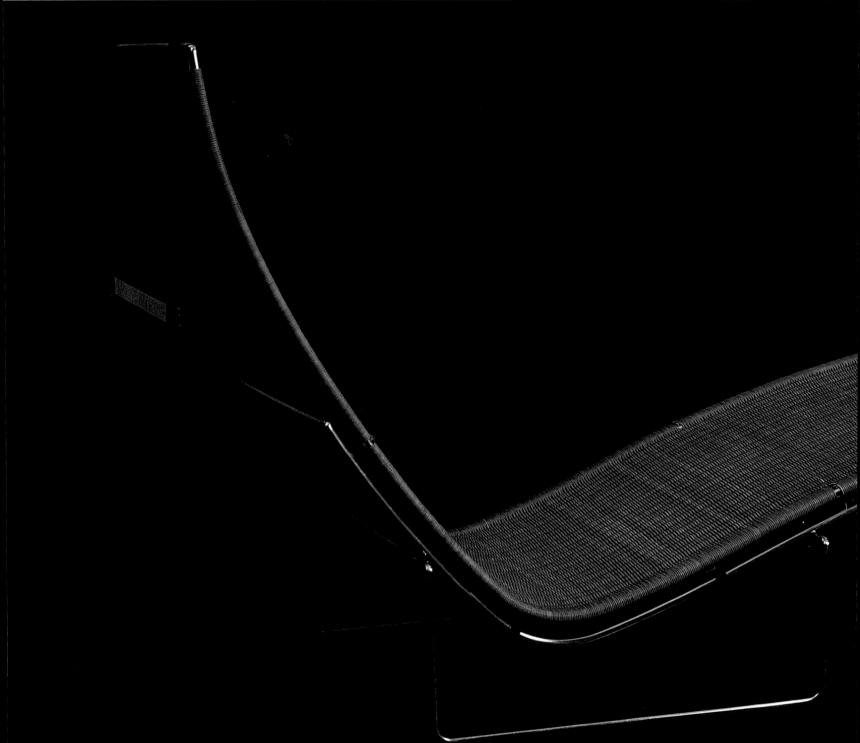

around which space now had to be reorganized. Also, owing to high construction costs, the development of inexpensive furniture became an imperative.

A company set up by Ingvar Kamprad in 1943 originally as a hardware store was being overhauled: in 1950, a furniture range was introduced, with a catalog following in 1951. Kamprad had opened a shop in Almhult in 1953, but it was only in 1965 that outlets appeared in Stockholm, where, for the first time, ready-to-assemble furniture could be purchased self-service in flat-packs. This was Ikea, destined to become the emporium for the everyman, with typical Scandinavian products in oiled teak, woven curtains and netting, and the Ogda chair, a reinterpretation of the Thonet chair (still in the catalog), all very reasonably priced. In 1960s Sweden much thought was given to the needs of users, and, more particularly, to the disabled, as attested by the achievements of the Ergonomi Designgruppen and A&E Design.

Without a doubt, the most original design came from Finland. Like the Americans, the Finns, in a relatively new, liberated, democratic, and egalitarian country, were propounding the concept of "lifestyle." During the 1960s, Finnish designers such as Eero Aarnio, Yrjo Kukkapuro, and Marimekko began appropriating the prevailing pop culture. Surely one of the reasons underlying the originality of Finland was the fact that its creativity grew out of a still vital folkloric tradition: while the shapes were changing, the spirit remained the same.

In Finland, Denmark, and Sweden, the furniture industry represented a substantial proportion of GNP. A good example is Marimekko. Antti Nurmesniemi produced a steel and leather chair that was acquired by the Museum of Modern Art in 1964 as an example of the harmonious treatment of the predominant materials of the decade. Scandinavia possessed cooperatives affiliating users, industrialists/manufacturers, and distributors that backed the growth of the modern furniture industry. Scandinavian influence on European furniture was considerable, while Nordic designers were responsible for some of the most elegant creations in International Modernism.

Saburo Inui, Ply-Chair, 1960.
Natural maple plywood.
Tendo Mokko.
Courtesy Tendo Co., Ltd.,
Tendo Yamagata.

Reiko Tanabe, stool, 1960.
Molded teak plywood.
Tendo Mokko.
Courtesy Tendo Co., Ltd.,
Tendo Yamagata.

Japanese design

As it turned out, Scandinavian furniture exerted a far from negligible influence on Japanese design, in particular through exhibitions in department stores. In 1952, twenty-five members of the design community, among them Tatsuko Sasaki, Jiro Kosugi, Sori Yanagi, and Riki Watanabe, founded the Japanese Independent Designers Association (JIDA). Backed by the *Mainichi Shimbun* newspaper, they put on the first Japanese design competition. In 1960, the World Design Conference (WoDeCo) was held in Tokyo, giving Japanese design the seal of approval.

One of the most forward-looking initiatives belonged to the Tendo Mokko company. Established in 1940 at Tendo as a cooperative, this association united carpenters and cabinetmakers from all over the city and won contracts with the Japanese army. Towards the end of World War II, it began exploring

Kenji Fujimori, chair, 1961.
Keyaki plywood.
Tendo Mokko.
Courtesy Tendo Co., Ltd.,
Tendo Yamagata.

Isamu Kenmochi, chair. 1961.
Molded maple plywood,
metal legs.
Tendo Mokko.
Courtesy Tendo Co. Ltd.,
Tendo Yamagata.

Kenzo Tange, Olympic
Stadium, Osaka, 1970.

TV8-301, first transistor
TV set, 1960.
Sony.

the potential of shaping wood and
to this end employed bentwood
techniques. The firm turned its interest
to plywood, well-adapted for aviation,
and adopted a technique of ply-molding
that applied the electromagnetic pulses
used in radar to generate the heat
required. It was at this juncture,
Isamu Kenmochi and Tendo Mokko
collaborated. Purchasing a high-
frequency generator and thermal
presses, the company adapted the
technology to contemporary furniture.
The pieces created were shown at the
Takashiyama department store in Tokyo.
Tendo then opened a branch in the
capital and began production of a series
in plywood following an order of

4,500 seats for the stadium in the
Shizuoka prefecture built by Kenzo
Tange. In 1960, in celebration of its
twentieth anniversary, Tendo Mokko
sponsored the very first furniture design
competition, with first prize going
to Reiko Tanabe's stool.

After 1960, responsibility for design
fell to independent designers who
benefited from an economic boom
that brought with it the opening of
numerous new hotels. Isamu Kenmochi
fitted out the New Japan Hotel in Tokyo,
showing his refined color sense in the
painting of its darkened, smoked walls.
The dining room was furnished with
cane furniture and dividers in *tsuzure-
ori* fabric, while the walls were adorned

Shiro Kuramata,
Pyramid unit, 1968.
Black and transparent
extruded plastic.
Ishimaru Co., Ltd.
Photo: Takayuki Ogawa.

Daisaku Choh, plywood
chairs, 1960. Japanese
oak veneer, upholstered
seat, fabric cover.
Tendo Mokko, Tendo.
Courtesy Design Center
Nagoya.

with calligraphy. Kenmochi was also
the designer of the Kashewado chair.
Sori Yanagi designed the Butterfly stool
(1956); Kenji Kijimori, a tatami seat;
and Daisaku Choh, a low-slung chair.
The chair was without antecedents in
Japan—save perhaps for the nobility's
folding stools.

Isamu Kenmochi,
coffee table with
incurving feet, 1968.
Rosewood.
Tendo Mokko.
Courtesy Tendo Co. Ltd.,
Tendo Yamagata.

The Modern Movement in Italy

Olivetti. Industry is a force that leaves an indelible mark on those natural, human, and social landscapes in which it elects to take root. Its products transform how we think and live, and play a part in cultural change. Olivetti's strength resided in understanding that it had to be ready to update its image constantly and interact with a real, dynamic world. In this sense, the demands of the art known as industrial design had priority over those of marketing. Designers have to operate on two levels at the same time: they need to express their talents as designers, in which personality fulfills a role, and they have to respect the pact with the machine, the manufacturing industry, and the end user.

Olivetti's debut showroom in Paris was fitted out by Gae Aulenti, with Carlo Scarpa doing the one in Venice, and Hans von Klier that in Turin. Similar care was taken over exhibition stands, the preeminent meeting place for an industry and its public. For these, Olivetti chose figures like Aulenti, Ettore Sottsass, Jr., and Walter Ballmer. Olivetti's flourishing partnership with Ettore Sottsass kicked off in 1958. It was Sottsass who designed the first Italian computer, the Elea 9003 (1959), in the process creating a whole new dimension, a new family of shapes— the world of electronics. He produced the Praxis 48 typewriter (1964) and introduced color for the Valentine portable typewriter (1969) made of red ABS. Rodolfo Bonetto joined Olivetti in the machine-tool design sector. Mario Bellini then joined the team, coming up with the magnetic character encoder CMC7 (1963) and the Programma 101 calculator (1965).

Mario Bellini, showroom display for Cassina, 1969. Courtesy Mario Bellini Associati, Milan.

Ettore Sottsass, Valentine portable typewriter. Injection-molded ABS casing, metal. Manufactured in collaboration with Perry A. King. Courtesy CNAC/MNAM. Photo: Jean-Claude Planchet.

Gio Ponti, furniture
created for the Parco
dei Principi Hotel,
Rome, 1964.
Courtesy Frank Rogin Inc.,
New York.

Osvaldo Borsani and
Eugenio Gerli, Graphis
series, 1968. Laminate top,
"L-shaped" base in
varnished steel.
Courtesy Tecno, Milan.
Photo: Pietro Carrieri.

Facing page: Classic
apartment decorated
by David Hicks, 1969.
Photo: Pascal Hinous.

Apartment and furniture
designed by Carla Venosta,
1967. Dining room with
metal partitions and
stainless steel furniture.
Photo: Pascal Hinous.

Classic apartment
decorated by
David Hicks, 1969.
Photo: Pascal Hinous.

Osvaldo Borsani,
hat stand AT 16, 1961.
Tecno, Milan.
Courtesy Tecno, Milan.

Oswaldo Borsani,
page 24 armchair, 1960.
Tecno, Milan.
Courtesy Tecno, Milan.

Achille Castiglioni,
Rampa multifunction
mobile storage, 1965.
Bernini, Milan.
Courtesy Studio
Castiglioni, Milan.

Achille Castiglioni,
Primate chair,
kneeling stool, 1970.
Zanotta, Milan.
Courtesy Studio
Castiglioni, Milan.

Facing page:
Achille Castiglioni,
Arco standard lamp, 1962.
Steel attached to
a block of Carrara marble.
Flos. Courtesy Studio
Castiglioni, Milan.

Library and reading area
with furniture designed
by Colin Morrow for an
apartment in Rome, 1971.
Photo: Pascal Hinous.

Facing page:
Achille Castiglioni and
Pier Giacomo Castiglioni,
Sanluca easy chair, 1961.
Courtesy Bernini, Milan.

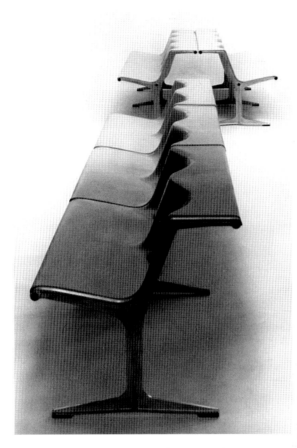

Friso Kramer, Banksystem 120, 1970. Dual seat, reinforced fiberglass shell, steel base. Courtesy Wilkhahn, Bad Münder.

Georg Leowald, model 230 office chair on casters, 1967. Édition Wilkhahn, Bad Münder. Courtesy Wilkhahn, Bad Münder.

Facing page: Delta Design, Programm 2000, office chairs, 1968. Fiberglass-reinforced polyester, leather covers. Édition Wilkhahn, Bad Münder. Courtesy Wilkhahn, Bad Münder.

New Marketing,
New Targets:
Popular Design

First *Prisunic* catalog,
April 1968, breakfast
corner by Terence Conran.
Prisunic catalog,
October 1969, Tubes
furniture by Gae Aulenti.
Prisunic catalog, April 1969,
Carpet divan
by Olivier Mourgue.

Facing page: Ahti Taskinen,
Puzzle sofa, 1968.
Wooden frame upholstered
in Marimekko
patterned fabric, 1968.
Courtesy Ahti Taskinen.
Photo: Mauno Viljakainen.

Modular foam
bucket-chairs.
Ikea. Courtesy Ikea, Paris.

After the austerity of postwar
reconstruction, the 1960s was a boom
time. The moment had come to
concentrate on sales strategies and
rethink tools adapted to the task at hand.

Francis Bruguière started working
for France's Prisunic in 1962 and, by 1964,
had become a furniture buyer.
At the time he was dealing in plastic
tablecloths, lace curtains, and cretonne
scatter cushions by the ton. He developed
a distribution network whose sales
catalog was inspired by the Camif and
the Coop, though there were differences.
Prisunic's strong point was packaging.
Bruguière decided to commission
designers. The then style director, Denise
Fayolle, suggested that Bruguière go and
see what was happening at Habitat.
In London, he met with Terence Conran
to whom he suggested creating

a furniture line for Prisunic, an offer
that was taken up in time for a launch
catalog that was distributed throughout
the chain. Orders were taken and sent on
to the manufacturer for delivery direct
to the customer. To work for Prisunic
was to cater to the general public, to
make design available to the greatest
number—the firm dealt in cash-and-
carry furniture as well as in a host of
other commodities.

The first catalog on which Terence
Conran collaborated is dated April 1968.
In it one reads: "Prisunic here presents
exclusive creations by the young
designer Terence Conran, who is also
a producer and owner of the Habitat
stores in London; this fusion of creation
and distribution furthers our awareness
of client needs and allows them to
be adapted to more swiftly. The Conran

style is currently the best representative of moderately priced, modern, rational, attractive furniture. One distinctive feature is the extreme diversity of use: the majority of these pieces are suited to many different purposes, rooms, and age groups." Exclusive models by Conran appear in the 1969 Prisunic catalog next to creations by a new face at Prisunic, Olivier Mourgue. This concentration on youth and innovation not only made itself felt in the area of furniture, but also applied to everything to do with interior decoration and homemaking—from carpets to electric appliances. Finally, Prisunic was conscious of the increasing importance in modern life of the notion of escape: the weekend, the country house, and outdoor activities. Catalog number three of the same year, *Decoration and Comfort in the Home*, also listed architect Gae Aulenti's "tube" furniture as well as pieces for children. The Prisunic/4 edition presented elements for contemporary interiors conceived by designers such as Gae Aulenti, P. Bacou, Terence Conran,

Jean-Pierre Garrault, Marc Held, Olivier Mourgue, and J.-C. Muller, available in novel materials, such as molded polyester, polyurethane foam, and vinyl. In 1969, reacting to the meteoric success of the Prisunic catalog, Francis Bruguière opened a 580-square-foot (54-square-meter) store that was to be

the chain's generic furniture space. Turnover was considerable and the brand remained faithful to its system until catalog number nine in 1973, when Bruguière found that the distribution system was no longer up to scratch and decided to open a store. He contacted Conran, who offered him the chance to

Tubular metal
and canvas chair.
Ikea.
Courtesy Ikea, Paris.

**Erik Wortz, Grabo sofa, 1964.
Courtesy Ikea, Paris.**

**Melamine end tables
on casters. Ikea.
Courtesy Ikea, Paris.**

launch Habitat in France. In 1972, he
accepted this proposal and left Prisunic.

Cash-and-Carry Retail

The forerunner of this system was
the Ikea store in Sweden. Kamprad's
brainchild had developed an
unprecedented retail vision: fixtures
are displayed to prospective customers
ready-mounted, accompanied by
suggestions for combining them and
for interior decor. The furniture items,
which for the most part can be
dismantled, are sold out of storage
areas in which customers help
themselves, like in a warehouse, before
proceeding to checkout. A similar retail
concept was embraced by Terence
Conran when he established Habitat
in 1964, with outlets functioning like
warehouses where furnishings are sold
on a carryout basis. In France, the
first Habitat store was opened
in Montparnasse in 1973 and covered
a surface area of 18,000 square feet
(1,700 square meters). The choice of
designers, however, was less extensive.

Office interior by Gallet with sculptural furniture, c. 1970. Photo: Pascal Hinous.

Facing page: Jonathan De Pas, Donato D'Urbino, Paolo Lomazzi, and Carla Scolari, Joe Di Maggio chair, expanded foam padding over metal structure, leather upholstery, 1970. Courtesy Galerie Down Town, Paris. Photo: Jacques Delacroix.

the "anti-object":
the poetry of forms

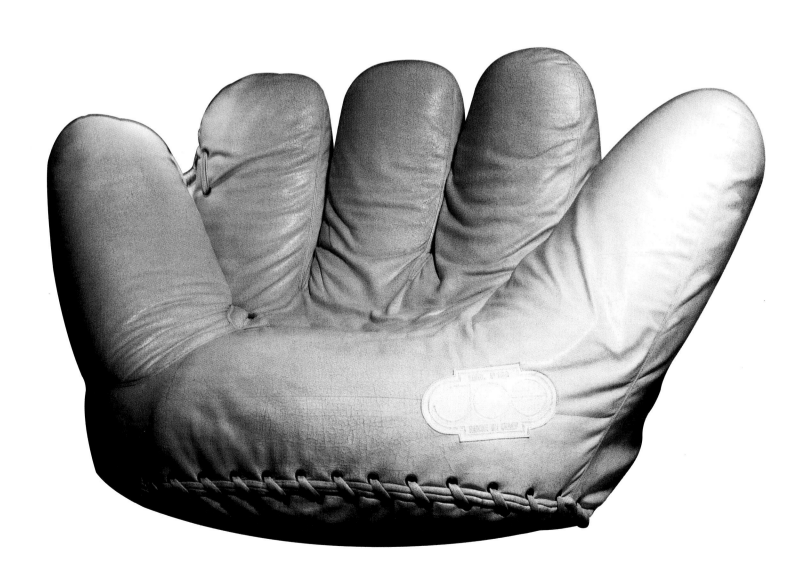

Space as Statement and "Anti-Design"
Rethinking the Object

Marcel Duchamp's long line of provocative acts left an enduring mark on the twentieth century: after flirting with Futurism, in 1915 he anticipated the Dada movement; with the idea of the readymade, he "hijacked" everyday objects, such as a bottle-drier or urinal, and displayed them as works of art. He inspired the Surrealists. At the 1938 World's Fair, Duchamp exhibited a "coal-sack" ceiling, while similar creative acts made him a harbinger of poetic and audacious ideas centering on the object. This immense genius died in Paris on October 1, 1968, leaving behind him a whole generation that saw him as both a precursor and a theorist of the "anti-object".

The question "What is design?" has dogged theorists and designers alike. Was it a blockbuster production bankrolled by an industry unsure whether it had the stomach for greater adventure? Was it "Functionalism," which certainly existed, but which had its roots in the 1930s? Duchamp had blazed an alternative path that now seemed worth exploring: his analysis of the object was liberated from preconceptions, but factored in something new by introducing psychology into daily life. It might lift the lid on a period that remained in the thrall of consumerism and pave the way for an irrational language, for an invitation to dream or write manifestos.

The debates, student revolts, and anti-capitalist protest movements of May 1968; a far from certain future; serious global conflicts; totalitarian ideologies—it is these, surely, that were behind the growing challenge to the object. And last but not least there was the spirit of participation, that sense of commitment: "living theater," "happenings," questions from the floor—stepping-stones to a more defiant creative stance. The meeting between art and technology in Kinetic Art; the direct appropriation of reality

Facing page: Günter Beltzig, Floris chair, 1967. Fiberglass-reinforced molded polyester. Wuppertal. Courtesy Galerie de Casson Méron, Paris.

Piero Gilardi, Sedilsasso, Sassi, painted "rocks" in polyurethane foam, 1968. Gufram, Balangero. Courtesy Gufram, Balangero.

Archizoom, Safari sofa, 1968.
Four elements in fiberglass-
reinforced polyester,
polyurethane-foam stuffed
seats novelty fabric covers.
Poltronova, Montale.
Courtesy Poltronova,
Montale.

of Nouveau Réalisme—with its "compressions," "accumulations," "packages"; the expressiveness of welded metal; the "shooting performances," feminist icons, lumino-kinetic, spatio-dynamic semiology (with Nicolas Schöffer's *Chronodynamism*), etc.: all new ideas that posited the language of art as a metaphor for an urban, industrial, and mass-media "nature." Arman exhibits armchairs burnt to a crisp to give vent to his rage against bourgeois comfort; in May 1963, a "package" by Christo deprives objects of all functionality. Christo had arrived in Paris in 1958 and was soon erecting a temporary construction on rue Visconti—a pile of oil drums that blocked the entire width of the street. Christo's ambition was to wrap buildings, but he tackled various objects before working on the *Corridor Store Front* in New York. The specific dimensions of a façade are above

all a morphological proposition for architecture, whose purpose is to forge links between man and the sociological fabric of the city and thus create an organic environment, an original space.

The 1960s are studded with new departures related to the object: Yves Klein's monochromes, a sensation of the soul; François-Xavier Lalanne and his functional bestiary; César and his "television" against consumer society; Jean-Pierre Raynaud and his "psycho-objects" that stand precisely at the crossroads where psychological reality and everyday life intersect; Takis and his luminous signals; light research with Lucio Fontana, the master of the "slash," who was to collaborate with designers Nanda Vigo and Ettore Sottsass; Guy de Rougemont, a painter who also made artist's lamps and furniture; Allen Jones, an English Pop artist who produced a realistic series of

Giorgio Ceretti, Pietro
Derossi, and Ricardo Rosso,
Puffo stool, 1970. Painted
polyurethane foam.
Gufram, Balangero.
Courtesy Gufram,
Balangero.

Giorgio Ceretti, Pietro
Derossi, and Ricardo Rosso,
Pratone, 1971. Painted
polyurethane foam.
Gufram, Balangero.
Courtesy Gufram,
Balangero.

House designed and built
by Jean Daladier based
on a dome structure, 1970.
Photo: Pascal Hinous.

leather-clad fetish-girl sculptures that double up as tables and chairs.

In a foreword to the *Mythologies Quotidiennes* (Everyday Mythologies) exhibition in July–October 1964 at the Musée d'Art Moderne de la Ville de Paris, Gerard Gassiot-Talabot wrote, "After the preeminence of Abstract Expressionism and Lyric Abstraction, both sides of the Atlantic are experiencing a wave of 'objectivation.' Be it Nouveau Réalisme, with its wholehearted embrace of the object in the raw or Pop Art, with its uncompromising snapshots of daily life through processes often derived from the mass market … The stylistic excesses, the paroxysm of the object practiced by European Nouveaux Réalistes and American Neo-Dadaists, the deadpan concoctions of Pop Art and Constructive Kineticism all inform choices that seem to be leaving less and less leeway for the artist."

Three-dome house designed and built by Jean Daladier. Photo: Pascal Hinous.

Designer unknown, child's chair, c. 1970. Courtesy XXO, Romainville.

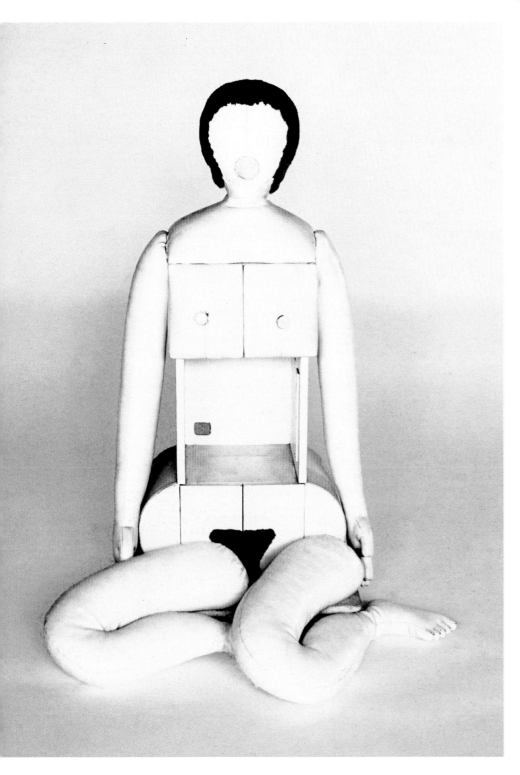

**Nicola, *Petite femme
télévision*, 1969.
Courtesy XXO, Romainville.**

Objet d'Art and Object Art

The 1962 exhibition, *L'Objet*, spearheaded
by François Mathey at the Musée des
Arts Décoratifs, provided one of the first
opportunities to interrogate the status
of the object. Products of the minds
of sculptors and painters, the objects
exhibited broke totally with the
tendencies of industrial design. Forever
in the forefront of developments in
architecture and the applied arts, these
artists had factored in all the diverse
parameters of the object and opened
up uncharted territory.

A few years later, in 1963, when
the issue was still a burning one, Michel
Ragon and Jacques Lacloche organized
an exhibition in a similar spirit entitled
*Furnished Studio Apartment, Place
Vendôme*. The exhibit space was handed
over to artists who appropriated both
interior design and furniture. Some time
later, jointly with François Mathey, they
extended their investigations on the
occasion of a new exhibition, *Objet 2*, at
the Galerie Lacloche, 8, place Vendôme.
The ambition this time was different
in that the object was not merely to
be an artistic tour de force: it had
to be capable of being reproduced—
a seat designed by an artist on which
one might actually sit down.

Artists literally transform the objects
they engage with. A "stylist" may
reconfigure an object; an artist endows
it with a whole new dimension: Picasso
with ceramics, Lurçat with tapestry,
Bertoia with chairs, Noguchi with
lighting—artists point the way
forward. *Objet 2* provided an arena in
which artists could see for themselves

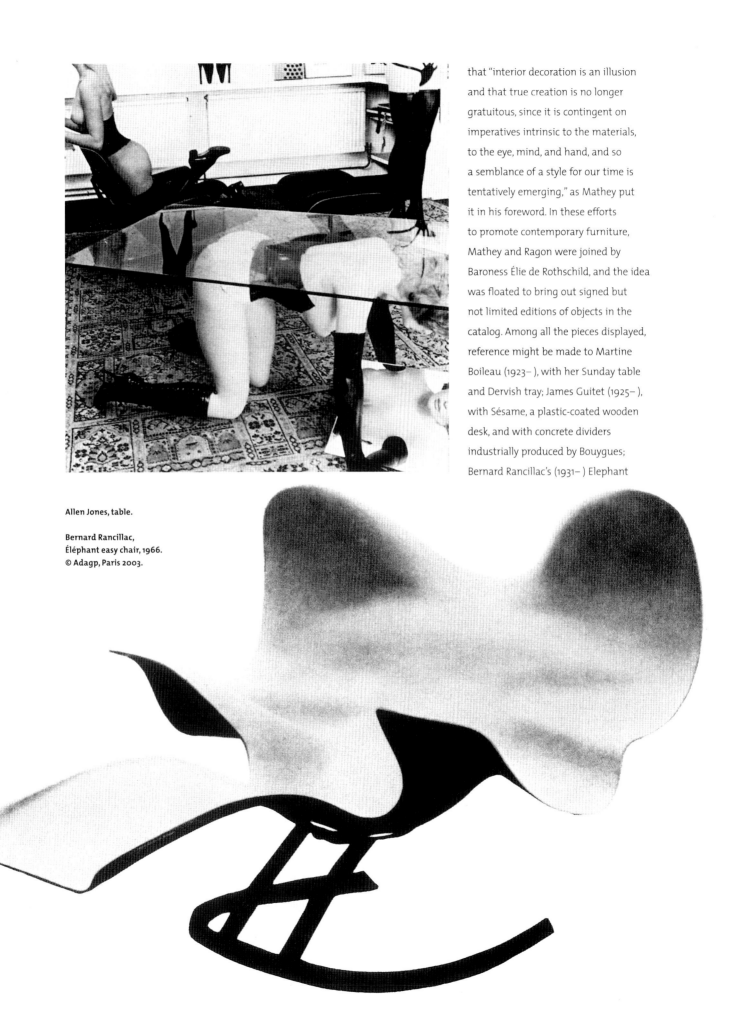

that "interior decoration is an illusion and that true creation is no longer gratuitous, since it is contingent on imperatives intrinsic to the materials, to the eye, mind, and hand, and so a semblance of a style for our time is tentatively emerging," as Mathey put it in his foreword. In these efforts to promote contemporary furniture, Mathey and Ragon were joined by Baroness Élie de Rothschild, and the idea was floated to bring out signed but not limited editions of objects in the catalog. Among all the pieces displayed, reference might be made to Martine Boileau (1923–), with her Sunday table and Dervish tray; James Guitet (1925–), with Sésame, a plastic-coated wooden desk, and with concrete dividers industrially produced by Bouygues; Bernard Rancillac's (1931–) Elephant

Allen Jones, table.

Bernard Rancillac,
Éléphant easy chair, 1966.
© Adagp, Paris 2003.

wing chair in molded polyester with metal-tubing base; Day Schnabel and a Blason table with built-in ashtray and brass magazine-rack; Arman's all steel and leather Spiral armchair; Georges Patrix, with a teak conference table; Roger Tallon, who presented a metamorphic plastic bed, as well as a portrait chair in molded plywood and the Métamorphoseur ceiling light; Philippe Hiquily, and an articulated wrought-iron table with separate wooden–glass–marble top. The majority of these designers were acknowledged artists, but some, such as George Patrix and Roger Tallon, hovered between two worlds, and were more engineers than artists.

Günther Beltzig, sculpted chair, c. 1970.

Nicola, Foot chaise longue. Vinyl. Collection Pierre Restany.

Ettore Sottsass Jr. (1917–). Like Joe Colombo, Sottsass belonged to the generation bridging the gap between prewar Italian pioneers and the new wave of designers, such as Andrea Branzi (1938–) and Alessandro Mendini (1931–). An architect by training and an inveterate traveler, he began working with his father. A consultant for Poltronova, and, by 1958, head of the electronics division at Olivetti, by the early 1960s, his approach had taken a more radical turn. His earliest non-realistic creations were ceramic objects, followed by anti-design furniture brought out by Poltronova. His investigations centered on childhood sensations and perceptions. He employed color to enhance designs

thought out as volumes rather than structures. Defining his own norms, Sottsass formulated a repertory of forms that might juggle ceramic and melamine-coated plastic, while his language was often inflected with signs conveying pre-existing iconographies from both art and popular tradition.

Memphis's new departures might be regarded as emerging from the explorations of anti-design. The Superboxes, closets designed in 1965 and featured in *Domus* in December 1965 and again in April 1967, do approximate furniture. Standing at the center of the room, and thus doing away with the need for walls, these monolithic objects open up the space, consolidate functions, and free daily life from

Ettore Sottsass, Grigi fiberglass furniture, 1970. The headboard contains two fluorescent lights. Poltronova, Montale. Courtesy Poltronova, Montale.

Ettore Sottsass, modular storage system. Poltronova, Montale. Courtesy Poltronova, Montale.

Facing page: Ettore Sottsass, Superbox Nirvana cupboard clad in colored melamine, 1966. Poltronova, Montale. Courtesy Poltronova, Montale.

routine. Sottsass's piece is not so much a "cupboard" as a multi-functional container open on the sides. His input extended to the color of the surrounding walls. Such furniture resembles a mirror onto a private existence and thus presents the personality of the individual to the external world. Sottsass baptizes his pieces: Gli Armadi Neri di Londra, Nirvana, Torno subito, Omaggio a Honda, L'Amatore del Magnetofono, La Camera di Hong Kong, La Camera col Tronco, Il Boudoir di Jean

Harlow, Maniglie Colorate, Harakiri dell'Architetto, I Like Sex, etc. Treating his cupboards as individuals, Sottsass painted on some of them a new language designed to focus concentration. If only a few of these creations were ever put into production, through them he was nevertheless able to develop exclusive models made by Abet Laminati, a company that manufactured melamine-coated plastics.

From the outset, Sottsass was supported in his efforts by Signor

Cammilli at Poltronova, which produced a range of furniture, mirrors, and lamps in ABS with psychedelic names. Owing to a lack of technical expertise, however, the collaboration petered out. The extraordinary contrast between this side of Sottsass's oeuvre and his work as an industrial designer—as manifested in Olivetti's Praxis 48 (1964), Tekne 3 (1964), Te 300 (1967), the Jukebox Audiovisual System (1969), or the Valentine portable typewriter (1969)—is astonishing.

From 1966 to 1972, the critique and analysis formulated by Sottsass (in tandem with radical architecture groups Archizoom and Superstudio) zeroed in on an autonomous "design utopia" aimed at an entirely imaginary customer, with both a sense of humor and a focus on life rather than business, that envisaged a craft renaissance as most likely to spring from the potential offered by new technologies. In 1969, with its projects for the No-Stop City, Superstudio offered a scientific analysis of the habitat problematic. The shift in perspective was defended by Andrea Branzi: "In Italy, we were stronger, more politically aware, we had more charismatic individuals, subtler minds. Whereas other foreign movements ended in an abyss, we tried to come up with long-term solutions, and our ideas broke new ground. It was against this backdrop that Alchymia, Memphis and, finally, Nuovo Design came into being."

Several anti-design groups flourished at this time, the most outstanding being Archizoom, followed by Superstudio and, finally, UFO, Gruppo Strum, and 9999.

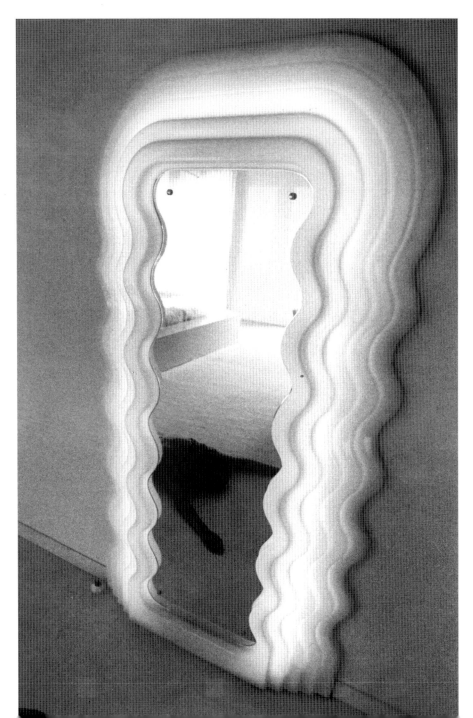

Facing page: Mario Bellini, Teneride polyurethane foam bucket chair, fiberglass swivel base, 1968. Cassina, Milan. Photo: Carol Marc Lavrillier.

Ettore Sottsass, Ultrafragola fiberglass mirror with integrated lighting, 1970. Poltronova, Montale. Courtesy Poltronova, Montale.

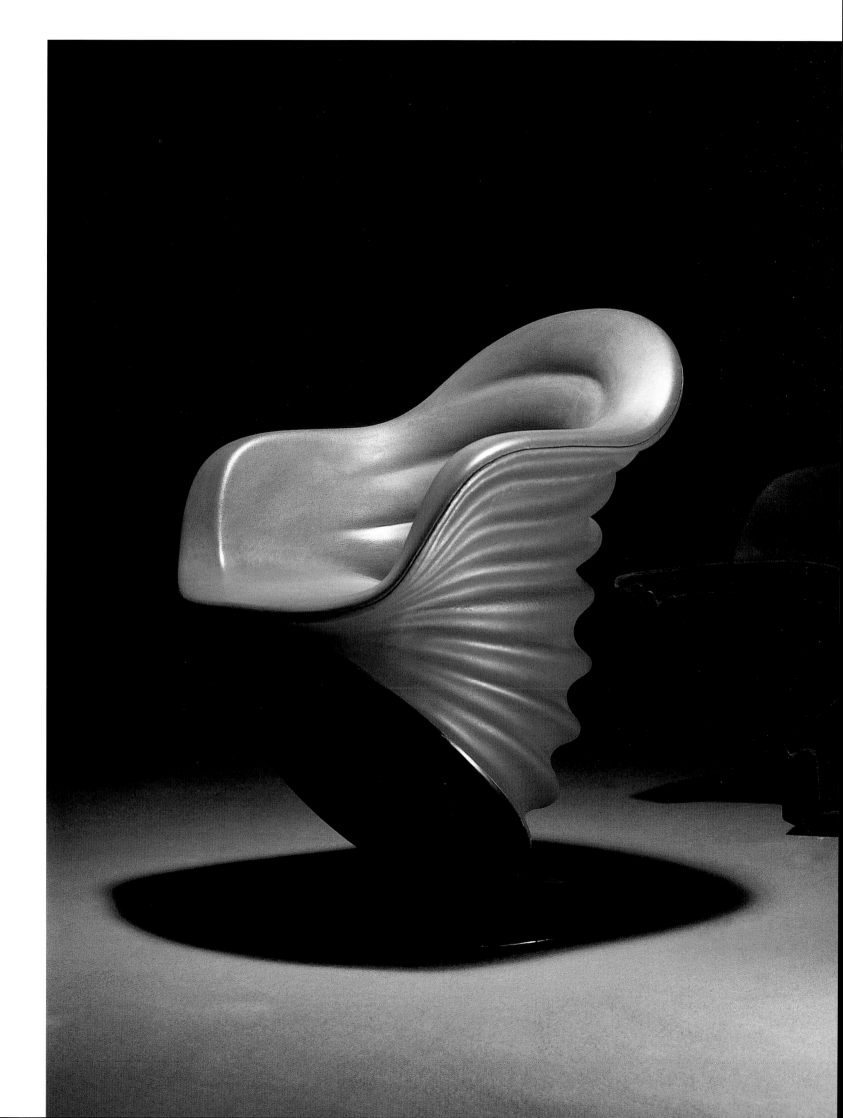

establishment of an "artists' city" at Sainte-Baume. Michel Tapié introduced him to the Stadler gallery. In 1960, Quentin's unstructured spaces morphed into swarms of written signs, counterdesigns, and outsized graffiti. He lived in Milan for two years and became friends with Lucio Fontana, Piero Manzoni, Enrico Castellani and joined up with Rotella, Klein, Spoerri, and Arman, who would all often visit the city. In 1961, he had a show in Turin and had begun to investigate machines (oscilloscopes, computers, etc.) at Olivetti before exhibiting work at Iris Clert's *Piccola Biennale* in Venice. He created his first inflatable structure, Cybule 1, at Pirelli's. After prolonged reflection and frequent discussions with Lucio Fontana, who

through "Spatialism" was advocating a broader conception of art liberated from the constraints of producing canvases, Quentin gave up painting entirely. In consequence, he increased the scale of his works and was against the art-dealer axis, devoting himself to transforming the environment through architecture/sculptures, monuments, design, and encouraging audience participation. In 1961, he designed a "faufauteuil" (fake easy chair), the Latex made by Pirelli in the same way as a tire inner tube. In 1962, he exhibited the full-scale model of the Croissant armchair at Adamoli, Varese. When it was mass-produced by Plasteco, the outsized model had to be rescaled. Quentin believed that painting's role was derisory in a civilization whose

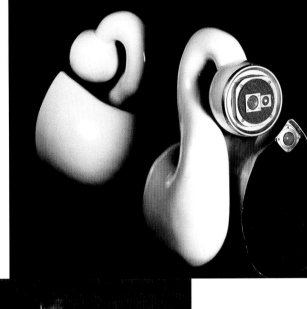

Designer unknown, radio, c. 1969. Courtesy XXO, Romainville.

Piotr Kowalski, *C'est pour tout de suite*, 1965.

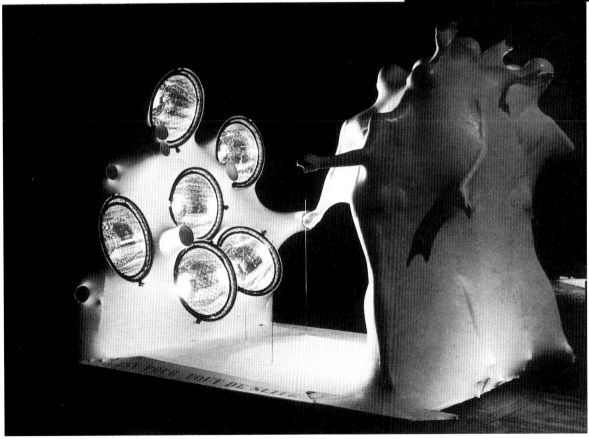

Bernard Quentin, inflatable
Croissant chair, 1966.
© Aérolande, Paris.
Photo: Vincent Freal & Cie.
© Adagp, Paris 2003.

visual communication landscape is dominated by television, comic strips, and film, and turned to making huge inflatable lettering structures, some six meters in height. He then created an inflatable chair with a water-filled base and a rod to strengthen the back. He left Italy, residing for two years in the United States, where he continued

to disseminate his ideas on the future of art. His arrival coincided, however, with the acme of the trend for Pop Art and a palpable hostility towards things Parisian. Overcoming various obstacles and hindrances, he managed to exhibit a pulsating inflatable structure with a preprogrammed "respiration cycle" (*Cybule III*, mural, 1963) at the World's

Fair, though it passed almost unnoticed. He drew encouragement, however, from Salvador Dalí, who saw in him a pioneer of cyber art and electronic writing. In spite of major misgivings about Pop Art, he became friends with both Lichtenstein and Warhol, as well as Duchamp, whom he had got to know through Arman (whose studio he was sharing at this time). In 1965, he made his way back to France, and then to Italy in 1966, where he continued his researches, producing other inflatable structures in PVC with Plasteco-Milano.

Quentin's inflatable environment was shown in New York again and met with greater success. Proceeding to Montreal, he there prepared a study for the French pavilion for the 1967 World's Fair with André Fougeron, hoping he might be able to build an inflatable superstructure for it. In 1967, he showed an inflatable environment in Neuilly, outside Paris, and revamped the Blow-Up Club in Milan. Back in Italy, in 1968 he investigated cardboard furniture, with the Nido d'Ape series of gray or black honeycomb forms, including ottoman, table, chairs, armchairs, and light fixtures. They were manufactured by Gavina of Bologna in small volumes. The unit, complicated in terms of cut, is held together by strips of Velcro. Gavina also produced furniture by other artists—Le Parc, Matta, Kuramata—that were shown in the Apollinaire gallery, Milan. Gavina then went bankrupt and the company was taken over by Knoll. Quentin made the Molecul'air seat, the outcome of his investigations into inflatable and molecular structures, before designing in Modena the body of a car that took part in the Le Mans Twenty-Four-Hour Race.

Quentin was aware of and approved of Aérolande's products. He was friends with Quasar but opted to produce his own furniture prototypes in opaque inflatable PVC, since he found that this added sculptural qualities to the piece, whereas Quasar preferred transparency. In Italy, he succeeded in exhibiting the Croissant in fluorescent pink PVC. In 1970, he unveiled an inflatable structure for the terrace of the French pavilion at the Osaka World's Fair, a space he had conceived of as a cultural forum to which he invited Jean Tinguely and Niki de Saint-Phalle. The architect was Fougeron, but the pavilion left something to be desired. The firm of Zodiac constructed the unit employing a "collage" technique and a soldering process that it had not entirely mastered.

Apartment designed by Claude Parent in accordance with the principles of *architecture oblique*, Neuilly, c. 1970. Photo: Gilles Ehrmann.

Claude Courtecuisse,
folding chairs with
occasional table
module, 1967.
Ondulys. Cardboard.
Courtesy Claude
Courtecuisse.

Jean-Louis Avril,
dining-room table
and chairs, 1967.
Cardboard.
Photo: Laurent
Sully Jaulmes.

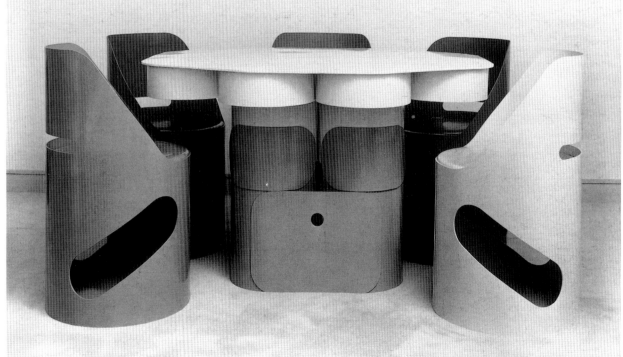

Guy de Rougemont,
Volumineux,
light sculpture
created in 1969.

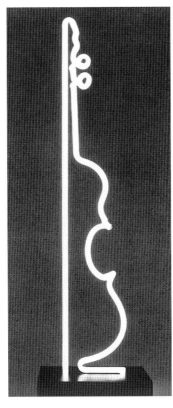
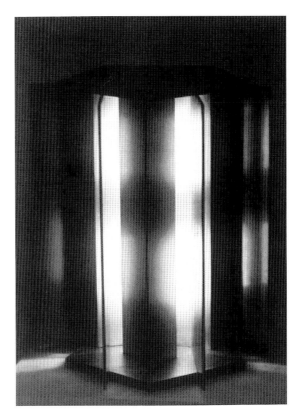

Arman, neon lamp, issued by Atelier A, c. 1967.

Jean-Paul Barray and Kim Moltzer, lighting unit, with a system of two pivoting surfaces, 1969.

André Caseneuve, light "stones," produced by Atelier A, c. 1967.

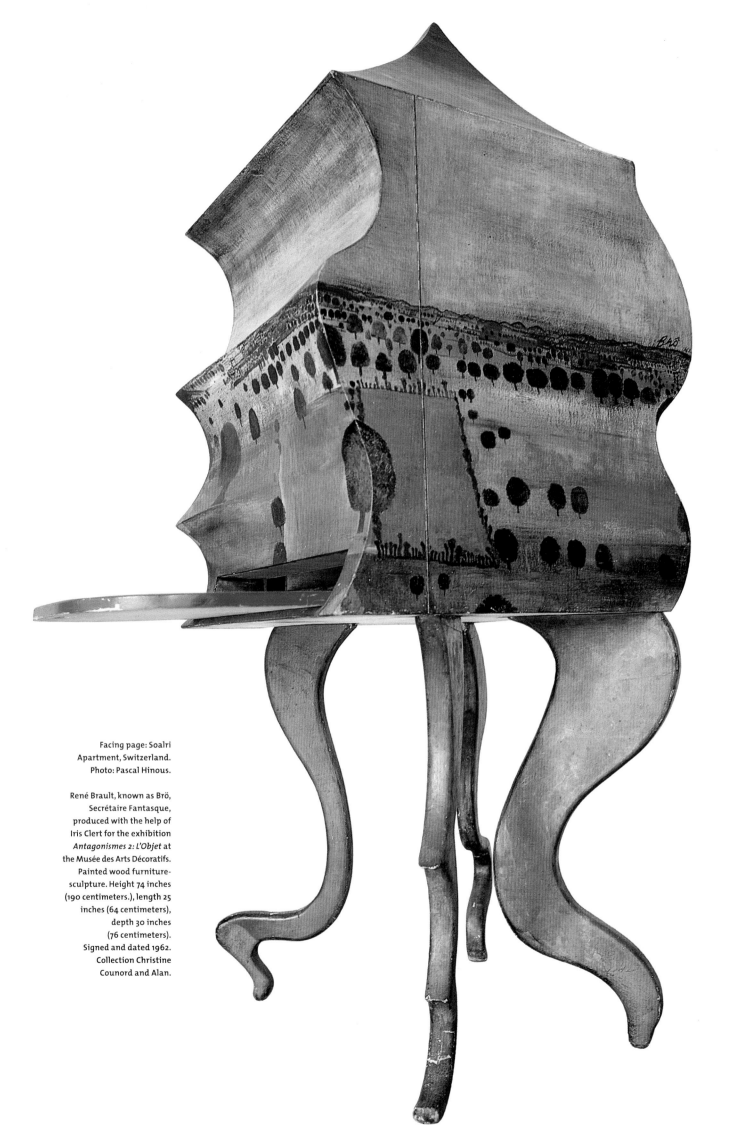

Facing page: Soalri
Apartment, Switzerland.
Photo: Pascal Hinous.

René Brault, known as Brö,
Secrétaire Fantasque,
produced with the help of
Iris Clert for the exhibition
Antagonismes 2: L'Objet at
the Musée des Arts Décoratifs.
Painted wood furniture-
sculpture. Height 74 inches
(190 centimeters.), length 25
inches (64 centimeters),
depth 30 inches
(76 centimeters).
Signed and dated 1962.
Collection Christine
Counord and Alan.

François Dallegret (1937–). A French-Canadian designer who trained at the École des Beaux-Arts in Paris, he debuted with an exhibition at Iris Clert's gallery entitled *Mechanical Drawings*. He created a vast array of utopian projects, including the Environment-Bubble, the Powermembrane House, the Transportable Living Package, and drew the illustrations for Reyner Banham's landmark article, "A Home is not a House." He produced accessories in the Klik series, shown for the first time in 1968 at the International Design Conference at Aspen. Then embarking on restaurant interiors, in Montreal in 1965 he fitted out the two-story Le Drug—an amalgam of drugstore, boutique, restaurant, gallery, and discotheque—that one entered after forcing a path through a complex sculpture of wire and chains, and, in 1970, Eat & Drink at the World Trade Center, New York. He was also the designer of the *Fleurs à vent*, multicolored, wind-powered structures that adorned the entrance to the Ronde on the site of the 1967 World's Fair in Montreal. One of Dallegret's chief concerns was the dialogue between art and technology, and his explorations led to his "machinations." In 1966, he developed Atomix, a mechanical system that could produce an infinite number of random images. He also produced a "spring chair," the Chaise-Ressort, in anodized aluminum (1969).

Archizoom chair,
Homage to Mies,
chromium tubular
structure, rubber seat
1967.
Poltronova, Montale.
Copyright, Gilberto Coretti.

Pierre Restany, *Self-portrait*,
neon lamp.
Private collection.

Facing page, top: François
Arnal, Formula 1 chaise
longue. Metal, wheels,
padding. Collection Frac
Ile-de-France.

Facing page, bottom:
Arman,
Tambour chair.

Limited Editions, Artists' Editions

Atelier A. François Arnal (1924–). As his
father worked as a wine grower near
Toulon in the South of France, Arnal
spent his early days on a tractor. He
possessed a precocious intuition for art,
however, when, for his mother's birthday,
he built a twenty-eight-inch-wide
(seventy-centimeter-wide), hundred-foot-
long (three-hundred-meter-long) path
out of bits of wood he had found in the
countryside. He became acquainted with
the art world only after World War II.
Considering himself primarily a painter,
even before his experiments with
Atelier A, he had nevertheless produced
furniture designs for the interior
designer Henri Samuel, who held his
efforts in high regard: it was for him that

Arnal designed furniture in Plexiglas, in particular the Propeller table. Believing art to be dead, after May 1968 the self-taught painter started making soft sculptures that people could use as chairs. It was probably this initial foray into Object Art that ultimately determined his path. Temporarily relinquishing painting, Arnal appealed to the artistic milieu he frequented for designs for objects or furniture, to which some responded with thumbnail sketches, while others presented detailed plans. Some forty artists were eventually to participate in Atelier A's venture: among others, François Arnal himself, Roy Adzak, Arman, Enrico Baj, Jean-Paul Barray, France Bertin (Nappe table), Mark Brusse, Gilles de Bure, André Cazenave, César, Dmitrienko, Degani, Pucci de Rossi, Ruth Francken, Alain Jaquet, Peter Klasen, Piotr Kowalski, Lionel Lebovici, Lourdes Castro, Malaval, Annette Messager, Miralda, Penseca, Pradalier, Jean-Pierre Raynaud, Pierre Restany, Sanejouand, Telemaque, Bernar Venet, and Viseux. The group's purpose was to educate the public and make it more receptive to artistic creativity by leaving the world of galleries and museums to which only an elite had access, and it saw its task as producing artist-designed objects and furniture. This commercial objective was complemented by a didactic purpose, with each object or piece of furniture accompanied by a presentation of the artist, a detailed biography in five or six languages, photographic documents, as well as the design for the project sold. The pieces produced by Atelier A were exhibited at many exhibitions, including

Jean-Michel Sanejouand,
Symmetric rocking chair.
Chromium-steel structure,
vinyl seat.
Collection François Arnal.
Photo: Vincent Leroux.

Pierre Paulin,
Arachnéen chair, 1965.
Artifort.

the Eurodomus in Turin and the Salon du Meuble in Paris. In business terms, the concern mounted by François Arnal was relatively significant, with from two to three draftsmen producing designs to precise technical criteria to facilitate development from basic idea to prototype. Arnal employed salesmen in the United States, Italy, and Belgium. Unfortunately, with neither market research nor publicity budget, the only support came from the specialized press. The company was soon posting a loss, and in 1975 Arnal filed for bankruptcy.

The experiment had lasted from 1969 to 1975, however, and 190 objects and pieces of furniture were manufactured, often in a single, unique edition. Arnal concentrated on furniture; Adzak and Mark Brusse produced the chairs. A unique experiment in the interaction between art and design, Atelier A acquired still greater legitimacy in January 1970, when Pierre Restany penned a mission statement that was translated into fifteen languages. The willingness of artists to take part in such adventures remained fragile, however, since they felt little inclination to forfeit their status as artists and refused to compromise themselves in the world of design (Annette Messager was a prime example). The environment at that time was quite different from the present, with designers circulating freely between disciplines.

Prior to Atelier A's ventures in France, a similar phenomenon had occurred in Italy—the Mana Art Market, a Rome-based concern that had exhibited "Multiples of Mana," the offshoot of an appeal by Nancy Marotta to artists of a poetic sensibility who did not normally deal in rationalized multiples of their work. This mutation of the artwork into a utilitarian, rational artifact affected all kinds of objects, attesting to the social concerns that informed many individual investigations. By the same token, it provided an arena in which sculpture might be treated functionally—though David Morris's Magic Couch can also be understood as primal sculpture. The application of artistic ideas to the realm of design gave rise both to the tools for realizing the objects concerned and the principles of their distribution. Examples of creations of this type include doors by Enrico Castellani and Luigi Fontana, a Perspex container by Gino Marotta, sofas by Gianni Colombo and Martial Raysse, the Giostra Magica sculpture-couch by David Morris, and a Dollar table by Franco Angeli.

**Roy Adzak, *Fesses* chair.
ABS cube.
Collection François Arnal.**

Conclusion

Fueled by the exploration of new types of space, by population growth, a favorable economic situation that fostered the emergence of more varied forms of behavior, the 1960s were essentially a decade of reflection and questioning, as well as of experimentation, exuberance, and excess. Many artists, architects and designers endeavored to frame solutions for the time ahead that would integrate new factors, such as the population explosion, the development of mass communication, the breakdown of traditional structures, and the attractions of a nomadic way of life.

Space and its scientific or imaginary exploration, together with science fiction, fed into many fields of creativity: art, comics, plays, and film (Roger Vadim's *Barbarella* in 1967 and Stanley Kubrick's *2001: a Space Odyssey* in 1968).

Young designers were to point the way to a world with a very different outlook: speed, transportation, and travel all acted as spurs to a new-found

conception of space-time. Designers, too, were asking questions. They created "housing cells" on an industrial scale. In 1968, the Finnish architect Matti Suuronen presented a highly successful project, the Futuro House, whose themes were characteristic of utopian architecture. Mobility is conveyed by its flying-saucer shape, leisure time by comfortable seating, and versatility by the transformability of the living area into a bed unit made of reinforced polyester.

In the course of his experiments on habitats that could diversify in relation

Quasar Khahn, two round armchairs viewed through the porthole in the cylindrical house, 1967. © Aérolande, Paris. Photo: Michel Moch.

Scene from *2001: A Space Odyssey*, by Stanley Kubrick, 1968.

Facing page: Jeanine Abraham and Dirk Jan Rol, Shell House presented at the Salon des Artistes Décorateurs in 1967. Courtesy Abraham and Rol.

to space-time, Joe Colombo devised two structures, Roto Living and the Closing Bed, deliberately reminiscent of machines or mega-household appliances that paid no heed to the canons of taste. Such structures had little to do with utopia: they existed, they possessed their own imperatives, and were able to adapt to all kinds of demands in terms of space and time brought to the fore by present-day housing conditions.

Nothing seemed impossible. In conjunction with the artist Nicolas Schöffer, Claude Parent (1923–) also encountered Utopia: after their project for a "spatio-dynamic" city came to naught, Parent developed his theory of the Maison Oblique for "off-center" living on his own. In this spirit, he fashioned an apartment for Andrée Bellaguet, the interior of which is laid out along oblique, dynamic lines, through a number of levels and spaces that allow the individual or group to move around as they pleased. One response to the problem of housing and mobility was the inflatable structure, transportable (house in a trunk, furniture in a bag)

and economical (inflatable partitions, furnishings, even plumbing). These ideas were extended by Jean-Paul Jungmann, Jean Aubert, and Antoine Stinco, in an experimental inflatable dwelling, the Dyodon. In 1968 during the *Structures Gonflables* (Inflatable Structures) event, Quasar (1934–) exhibited a cylindrical inflatable house mounted vertically in elements on a circular base with a floor and girded by a "doughnut," the whole covered by an inflatable circular lens. The entire unit was constructed out of see-through PVC. "Liberated from the weight of matter, from the weight of accepted ideas … a free man is better: this is the man of tomorrow," proclaimed Quasar in *Architecture d'aujourd'hui* (April–May 1971, p. 60).

In 1968, the West was sent reeling by a generation in revolt against the consumer society and waste. This floodtide of protest invaded industrial wastelands with their lofts and untreated concrete. In its drive to reject the superfluous and concentrate on essentials, fashion was scorned and

the watchword became basic forms.

A forerunner of "high-tech" style, a new spirit was surfacing. Embodying its commitment to recycling industrially produced elements, it was to become widely popular in the following decade. In the same years, the Hippie movement expressed a growing awareness of the power of Nature, its fascination, its simple rules, its lack of taboos— and of its critical vulnerability.

Against the background of this "soft" militancy that paved the way for ecological battles to come and for the "alternative" lifestyle trend, May 1969 saw the setting up of an ecological and solar community, the Cosanti Foundation, in Scottsdale, Arizona. It was slowly but surely dawning on some that the consumer boom was not going to last forever, and there were telltale signs of major crises to come. In 1973, came the first oil crisis, sounding the end of the predominance of plastics and synthetic materials. Confronted by stark new realities, the 1970s heralded the era of rationalism and contingency to come.

Bibliography

Amic, Yolande. *Le Mobilier français
1945–1964*. Paris: Éditions du
Regard/VIA, 1983.

*Austerity to Affluence: British Art and
Design, 1945-62*. London: Merrel
Holberton, 1997.

Barré, François and Jacques Beauffet.
*Design et quoi ? Histoire d'une
collection*. Lyon: Artha, 2002.

Beazley, Mitchell. *Robin and Lucienne
Day: Pioneers of Contemporary Design*.
London: Octopus Publishing, 2001.

Branzi, Andrea. *The Hot House: Italian
New Wave Design*. London: Thames &
Hudson, 1984.

Brunhammer, Yvonne. *Le Mobilier
français 1930–1960*. Paris: Éditions
Massin, 1997.

Brunhammer, Yvonne and Marie-Laure
Perrin. *Le Mobilier français 1960–1998*.
Paris: Éditions Massin, 1998.

Bure, Gilles de and Chloé Braunstein.
Tallon. Paris: Éditions Dis voir, 1999.

Conran, Terence. *Terence Conran Design*.
Gründ, 1997.

*Contemporary Furniture: an
International Review of Modern
Architecture, 1950 to the Present*.
London: The Design Council, 1982.

Design japonais 1950–1995. Paris:
Éditions du Centre Pompidou, 1995.

Dietsch, Deborah K. *Classic Modern:
Mid-Century Modern at Home*. New
York: Simon & Schuster, 2000.

*La Donation Vicky Remy. Une idée
de l'art pendant les années 70,
la rigueur et la rupture* . Saint-Étienne:
Éditions MAM Saint-Étienne,
1993.

Eidelberg, Martin. *Design 1935–1965:
What Modern Was?* New York: Harry N.
Abrams, 1991.

Fairbanks, Jonathan L. and Elizabeth
Bidwell Bates. *American Furniture 1620
to the Present*. Washington: Library of
Congress, 1981.

Favata, Ignazia. *Joe Colombo and Italian
Design of the Sixties*. London: Thames
& Hudson, 1988.

Fiell, Charlotte and Peter Fiell. *Modern
Furniture Classics: Postwar to Post-
Modernism*. London: Thames &
Hudson, 2001.

Fiell, Charlotte and Peter Fiell. *1000
Chairs*. Cologne: Taschen, 1997.

*From Ellen Key to Ikea, a Brief Journey
Through the History of Everyday
Articles in the 20th Century*. The Röhss
Museum of Arts and Crafts, 1991.

Garner, Philippe. *Les Arts décoratifs
1940–1980*. Paris: Bordas, 1982.

Garner, Philippe. *Sixties Design*. Cologne:
Taschen, 2001.

Greenberg, Cara. *Op to Pop: Furniture of
the 60s*. Boston: Little, Brown & Co.,
1999.

Grinfeder, M. H. *Les Années supports
surfaces 1965–1990*. Paris: Herscher,
1991.

*The Inflatable Moment: Pneumatics
Protest & Protest in 1968*. New York:
Princeton Architectural Press
Publishing.

Kron, Joan and Suzanne Slesin. *High
Tech: the Industrial Style and Source
Book for the Home*. Harmondsworth:
Penguin Books, 1978.

Lazzaroni, Laura. *35 Years of Design at
Salone del Mobile 1961–1996*. Milan:
Cosmit.

Made in Paper. Museum of
Contemporary Crafts, 1967.

Maillard, Robert, ed. *25 ans d'art en
France 1960–1985*. Paris: Larousse, 1986.

Popper, Frank. *Art-Action and
Participation*. London: Studio Vista,
1975.

Radice, Barbara. *Ettore Sottsass: a Critical
Biography*. New York: Rizzoli, 1993.

Raimondi, Giuseppe. *Italian Living
Design: Three Decades of Interiors*.
London: Tauris Parke Books, 1990.

Renous, Pascal. *Portraits de décorateurs*.
Paris: H. Vial, 1969.

Restany, Pierre, *60/90—Trente ans du
nouveau réalisme*. Paris: La Différence,
1990.

Roger Tallon à Vallauris. Nice: Grégoire
Gardette Éditions, 2001.

Sutherland, Lyall. *Hille—75 years of
British Furniture*. Elron Press Ltd., 1981.

Taragin, Davira S., Edward S. Cooke, and
Joseph Giovannini. *Furniture by
Wendell Castle*. New York: Hudson Hills
Press, 1989.

Tutino Vercelloni, Isa. *Années 60, design
retrouvé*. Milan: Artemide, 1999.

*Les Visionnaires de l'architecture,
Balladur, Friedman, Jonas, Maymont,
Ragon, Schöffer*. Paris: Robert Laffont,
1965.

*Vital Forms 1940–1960: American Art
and Design in the Atomic Age*. New
York: Harry N. Abrams, 2001.

Von Vegesack, Alexander and Mathias
Remmele. *Verner Panton: the Collected
Works*. Weil am Rhein: Vitra Design
Museum, 2000.

Watson, Anne. *Mod to Memphis Design
in Color 1960s–1980s*. Sydney:
Powerhouse Publishing, 2002.

Young, Dennis and Barbara Young.
Furniture in Britain Today. London:
Alec Tiranti, 1964.

EXHIBITION CATALOGS

Mathey, François, ed. *L'Objet 2*. Paris: Musée des Arts Décoratifs, 1962.

Formes utiles, 1963.

Formes industrielles. Paris: Musée des Arts Décoratifs, 1963.

Gassiot-Talabot, G. *Mythologies quotidiennes*. Paris: Musée d'Art Moderne de la Ville de Paris, 1964.

Formes utiles, 1965.

Amic, Yolande. *Les Assises du siège contemporain*. Paris: Musée des Arts Décoratifs, 1968.

Science-fiction. Paris: Musée des Arts Décoratifs, 1968.

Qu'est-ce que le design? Paris: CCI, 1969.

Pop art nouveau réalisme, Nieuwe Figuratie. Brussels: André de Rache, 1970.

Douze Ans d'art contemporain en France. Paris: Grand-Palais, 1972.

10 ans 100 modèles. Paris: CREAC, 1973.

Marc Held 10 ans de recherché. Nantes: Musée des Arts Décoratifs, 1974.

Matériau/technologie/forme. Paris: CCI, 1974.

Métamorphoses finlandaises. Paris: CCI, 1978.

Favata, Ignazia, ed. *Joe Colombo*. Musée d'Art Moderne de Villeneuve-d'Ascq, 1984.

Mobilier national 20 ans de creation. Paris: CCI, 1984.

Möbel Design: Made in Germany. Zentrum Baden-Wurttemberg, 1985.

Finn forma. Budapest: Iparmüvészeti Múzeum, 1988.

L'Objet-sculpture. Paris: JGM Galerie, 1990.

Hahne, Fritz. *Dokumente der Gestaltung*. Frankfurt: Rat für Formgebung, 1991.

Antti Nurmesniemi: to Reflect and to Design. Helsinki: Tamminiementie, 1992.

Pesce, Gaetano. *Le Temps des questions*. Paris: Éditions du Centre Pompidou, 1996.

Hvidberg-Hansen, Poul. *Dansk Moebel Design*. Trapholt, 1998.

Air Air. Monaco: Forum Grimaldi, 2000.

Perrigault, Pierre and Diane Saunier. *L'Architecte du mobilier 1950–2000—Rigueur et passion*. Meubles et fonction, 2000.

Schwarz, Rudolf. *More than Furniture, Wilkhahn—an Entreprise in its Time*. Verlag Form, 2000.

Francis, Mark, ed. *Les Années Pop 1958–1968*. Paris: Centre Pompidou, 2001.

M. Jousset, ed. La *Donation Kartell, un environnement plastique*. Paris: Éditions du Centre Pompidou, 2001.

Plaidoyer pour le mobilier contemporain, l'Atelier de recherche and de création du mobilier national (1964–2000). Galerie Nationale de Beauvais, 2001.

Mobili Italiani 61-91, le Varie eta dei Linguaggi. Milan: Cosmit.

Milan Triennale, French section, catalog 1968.

Salon des Artistes Décorateurs, catalogs 1961, 1963, 1965, 1967, and 1969.

Prisunic, *Catalogues*, 1, 2, 3, and 4.

Venice Biennale, 1996.

ARTICLES

"Doctrines," in *L'Architecture d'aujourd'hui*, October–November 1971.

"Le design," in *L'Architecture d'aujourd'hui*, April–May 1971.

"Interior Design Legends," in *Architectural Digest*, January 2000.

"Nelson, Eames, Girard, Propst, the Design Process at Herman Miller," in *Design Quarterly*, 98–99.

Connaissance des arts, 1965–1970.

Domus, 1960–1970.

Interni, 1966–1970.

L'Œil, 1966.

Maison française, 1960–1969.

MD, 1966.

Rivista dell'arredamento, 1960–1966.

Scandinavian Journal of Design History, November 2001.

Index

The publishers would like to express their thanks to the author Anne Bony.

They would also like to gratefully acknowledge all those who have been kind enough to assist her in her research and who have made this book possible:

Janine Abraham and Dirk Jan Rol, Jean-Paul Jungmann, Aérolande (Paris), François Arnal, Aake Anttila, Artifort (Schijndel), Farshid Assassi, Avarte Oy (Helsinki), Jean-Louis Avril, Giovanni Barengo Gardin, B&B Italia (Novedrate), Aldo Ballo, Marla C. Berns, Marc Berthier, Brionvega (Milan), Francis Bruguières, Serge Calka, Pietro Carrieri, Cassina (Milan), François Catroux, Gilberto Corretti, Claude Courtecuisse, François Dallegret, Agence Dallegret, Maria Wettergren, Galerie Dansk Moebelkunst (Paris), Galerie de Casson Méron, Jacques Delacroix, Nicolas Denis, Design Center Nagoya (Nagoya), John Davis, Design Council Slide Collection (Manchester), Die Neue Sammlung (Munich), Nanna Ditzel, Marc Domage, *Domus* (Milan), Galerie Down Town (Paris), Drouot-Presse (Paris), Gilles Ehrmann, Enzo Mari E Associati (Milan), Ole Jorgensen, Eric Jorgensen Mobelfabrik, Foto-Studio Casali (Milan), Frank Rogin Inc. (New York), Pierre Gautier-Delaye, Paul Genest, Gérard Grandval, Gufram (Balangero), Linda M. Baron, Herman Miller (Zeeland), Jim Norse, Hille (London), Pascal Hinous, Ikea (Paris), Grete Jalk, Françoise Jolant, Matthias Jousse, Jousse Entreprise (Paris), Kartell (Milan), Knoll (New York), Herbert Laessle, Carol Marc Lavrillier, Jacqueline Lecoq, Jean-Pierre Leloir, Elena Bellini, Mario Bellini Associati (Milan), Christine Sorin, MNAM/CCI (Paris), Madame Lerable, Mobilier National (Paris), Kim Moltzer, Lionel Morgaine, Michel Mortier, Olivier Mourgue, Georges Palot, Claude Parent, Pierre Perrigault, Gaetano Pesce, Jean-Claude Planchet, Francesca Balena Arista, Poltronova (Montale), Chloé Poracchia, Pulsi Photo, Philippe Recelle, Richard Schultz, Herbert Selldorf, Athi Taskinen, Studio Athi Taskinen (Finland), Studio Castiglioni (Milan), Ignazia Favata, Studio Joe Colombo (Milan), Laurent Sully Jaulmes, Roger Tallon, Tecno (Milan), Tendo Co. (Tendo Yamagata), Dorothée Thirion-Freiche, Coco Funabiki, Tokyo Design Center (Tokyo), Rina Troxler, Anne-Marie Valet, Verner Panton Design (Basle), Victoria & Albert Museum (London), Wilkahn (Bad Münder), Woods Studio, XXO (Romainville), Zanotta (Milan).

The author would like to take this opportunity of adding her expression of gratitude to that of her publishers.

All photographs by Pascal Hinous used here were taken for the magazine *Connaissance des arts,* Paris.

Translated from the French by David Radinowicz
Copyediting: Chrisoula Petridis
Typesetting: Thomas Gravemaker, Studio X-Act
Proofreading: B. Fernandez
Color Separation: Payton, Bilbao

Previously published in French as
Meubles et Décors des Années 60
© Editions du Regard, 2003
English-language edition
© Éditions Flammarion, 2004

www.editions.flammarion.com

04 05 06 4 3 2 1

FC0446-04-IV
ISBN: 2-0803-0446-1
Dépôt légal: 03/2004

Printed in Spain